Peter Wilding founded British Influence, the think tank for Britain's future in Europe, in 2012. He is a lawyer, speaker and writer on European politics and policy. Formerly Conservative European media chief and Sky's Europe Director, he is the author of *Influencing the European Union*, editor of the annual 'British Influence Scorecard' and one of the originators of the term Brexit.

'To achieve any grand strategy after a bruising campaign requires vision. I can think of few people more knowledgeable of Britain's tetchy relationship with Europe and therefore better able to sketch what that vision can be than Peter Wilding.'

–Vicky Pryce, former Joint Head of the UK Government's Economic Service

'In the ugly EU referendum campaign, the majority were persuaded to vote Leave in order that Britain might "take back control" of its destiny. In this stimulating book, Peter Wilding suggests that they had it back to front. Reviewing the sad history of our psychodrama with the European Union, he argues that Britain can best represent its own interests, and best contribute to the stability and prosperity of its neighbourhood, by the energetic deployment of its formidable assets behind a clear vision of Europe and of Britain's place in Europe.'

–Anthony Cary CMG, Commonwealth Scholarship Commissioner, former British High Commissioner to Canada and former British Ambassador to Sweden

'Peter Wilding thinks positively. Written from a ringside seat, his account of what's gone wrong, and how to put it right, makes timely and compelling reading.'

–John (Lord) Kerr, former Ambassador to the European Union, Ambassador to the United States, Permanent Under-Secretary at the Foreign Office and Head of the Diplomatic Service

'Peter Wilding's *What Next?* is a welcome overview of Britain's troubled and tumultuous relations with the rest of Europe, all the more welcome coming, as it does, just after a raucous and dispiriting referendum campaign. It reminds us that the essential part is to make a success of the follow-up on which Peter Wilding produces some thought-provoking ideas.'

–David (Lord) Hannay, former Ambassador to the European Union, Ambassador to the United Nations and author of *Britain's Quest for a Role: A Diplomatic Memoir from Europe to the UN*

'Peter Wilding's provocative take on Britain's complex relationship with the EU includes some profound historical analysis, especially on the European philosophies of Winston Churchill and Margaret Thatcher. He reminds us that both were, at least some of the time, passionately engaged prime ministers. Inspired by those two greats, Wilding sets out a patriotic and positive agenda for Britain.'

–Charles Grant, Director of the Centre for European Reform

WHAT NEXT?

Britain's Future in Europe

PETER WILDING

Published in 2017 by
I.B.Tauris & Co. Ltd
London • New York
www.ibtauris.com

ISBN: 978 1 78453 759 3
eISBN: 978 1 78672 113 6
ePDF: 978 1 78673 113 5

A full CIP record for this book is available from the British Library
A full CIP record is available from the Library of Congress

Library of Congress Catalog Card Number: available

Typeset by Riverside Publishing Solutions
Printed and bound in Great Britain by T.J. International, Padstow, Cornwall

Contents

Preface

In all the post-Brexit fog of war, neither the public nor our leaders should forget the sheer enormity of the choice Britain took on 23 June 2016. Brexit marks a transformation in the history of Britain, the EU and the European continent.

A new era, the third since the war, is opening up for Britain. After 1945 Britain sought influence in the world through the Empire. From 1956, after retreat from Suez, Britain sought leadership in Europe through what became the EU. But the 2016 withdrawal from the EU is different. After the war, Britain still led the Empire and, after Suez, joined Europe. Now it is year zero. No one knows what's next. And not just in the small print of new trade agreements. What does Brexit actually mean for Britain's place in the world? Where is the bigger picture?

With no Plan B, how can Britain still be a leader in Europe? Are we destined to tumble down the league table of international influence? Having been one of the EU's big three with France and Germany, what are the guidelines in British history that can point the way to the fresh start Britain has asked its leaders, if only by default, to choose? Boris Johnson has said 'We are leaving the EU, but not leaving Europe.' But what does that mean? What new path is open to Britain now and can past strategies give guidance?

It's partly my fault that the term Brexit entered the vocabulary so, in penance, this book tries to make some sense of it. Leavers believed the EU castrated British power and Remainers believed continued membership enhanced it. Neither wanted to diminish British clout and both sought a stronger Britain in the world. The referendum was, in fact, an often misguided debate about what it means to be patriotic. So while Brexit means leaving the present-day EU, it also means devising an imaginative settlement in Europe using all the influence and networks still at our disposal – a debate which this book tries to ignite. What Brexit does not mean is conducting a see-saw trench battle between stopping people coming and stopping business leaving, supercharged by online fact-wars, an approach which would repeat the failure of both sides' Gradgrindian fear campaigns. It would cheat the public of what they deserved during the referendum and need now: a bold and clear vision of Britain crafting a new place in Europe.

Lord Hennessy says: 'The referendum was like a lightning flash which illuminated a landscape that had long been changing. The country is fragmenting and I fear a fuse has been lit under the Union,' as well as Europe. Faced with such a historic task, the government cannot allow the Brexit debate to sit in the transactional furrow without, at the same time, charting a new course for an uneasy people.

It's high time. Despite championing the country – to the tune of £100 billion each year – our leaders now need to justify how great Britain really is. The nineteenth-century Swiss historian Jacob Burckhardt saw statecraft as a work of art. The danger of the post-Brexit world is that its leaders are colour-blind. If they don't think further and bigger outside the Brexit paintbox, the continental centrifugal forces at play, militarily, economically and politically, could threaten our security, prosperity and democracy. A new patriotism is needed.

My heartfelt thanks to all the staff and friends of British Influence who have been with us since we started in 2012. And I am delighted to acknowledge here the many Europewatch writers whose words and wisdom I have relied on in the production of this book.

Introduction

> England has saved herself by her exertions, and will, as I trust, save Europe by her example. It is necessary to form a treaty to which all the principal parties of Europe should bind themselves to protect and support each other as a general system of public law in Europe.
>
> (William Pitt the Younger, 1805)

> We had every Western European government ready to eat out of our hand in the immediate aftermath of war. For several years our prestige and influence were paramount and we could have stamped Europe as we wished. Jean Monnet and others on the continent had originally hoped to build a European economic union around the nucleus of a Franco-British union. It was the failure of the British to respond to this idea that led them to explore alternative approaches.
>
> (Sir Nicholas Henderson, 1979)

Could do better

In the premier league table of top countries where would Britain be? Battling for a place in the top four or a mid-table outfit? In 2015 an index of 'soft power' – the ability to lead through persuasion – ranked Britain as number one. China, 4 times as wealthy as Britain, 20 times as populous and 40 times as large, was facing relegation.[1]

The sun may have set on the British Empire, but this country finds itself with clout – a range of institutions and relationships in politics, economics, science and culture, often amassed over generations, which give it a great deal of internationally recognised influence.

Britain's power has far more to it than economics alone. Its cultural power is universal. Britain is a world-beater in global influence:

- It attracts more in foreign direct investment than Germany, France or Spain.
- Its capital, London, has overtaken New York as the premier global city.
- British citizens enjoy visa-free travel to 174 countries – the joint-highest of any nation.
- Its diplomats staff the largest number of permanent missions to multilateral organisations, alongside France.
- The royal family and the 'mother of parliaments' show to the world a stable, working democracy.
- It has 29 UNESCO World Heritage sites.
- It produces more internationally chart-topping music albums than any other country.
- Its football clubs have huge global support.
- Its universities are second only to those of the United States, attracting vast numbers of foreign students.
- The BBC successfully frames international events on British terms, broadcasting in every major language.
- The British Council, British Museum and other arts institutions make cultural contributions worldwide.

The UK could be said to have acquired a great many of these soft power assets 'in a fit of absence of mind', but the question this book poses and seeks to answer is whether the country has moved from absent-mindedness to neglect of its power. Is the seismic Brexit referendum vote of 23 June 2016 going to decrease that power and are we about to plunge down the league table of global influence?

Vladimir Putin certainly thinks so. The Russian President mocked Britain as a 'small island no one listens to'. This cannot be reconciled with the UK's position in the G7, the UN Security Council, NATO, in Europe and at the epicentre of the Commonwealth, but it is a view shared by a surprisingly large number of Britons. British Influence's polling showed that 61 per cent of British citizens want the UK to play a leadership role, confidently pulling the levers of global authority that we still have left to us. They want us to be the playground leader, not the surly loser in the corner. But 65 per cent believe that Britain has no influence and few if any friends. Sixty-six per cent believe that Britain is dominated at world level by the United States and that Europe is dominated by Germany and France. As far as they are concerned, Britain is a friendless loser in Europe, not a leader. Focus groups reveal that voters think Britain is 'insignificant', has 'lost its moral backbone' and 'has no vision'.[2]

How can this be so?

The reason for this 'victim syndrome' is that for 40 years the British have been strangers in Europe and, with the end of Empire, adrift in the world. Dean Acheson, who had been President Truman's secretary of state, hit below the belt in 1962 by saying that Britain had lost an empire and had not yet found a role. The problem is that Britain is still looking. Failure to articulate and act a visionary role has led to 50 years of foreign policy false starts.

With Brexit, the UK cannot simply proceed as before. It must change fundamentally the way it interacts with other nations and communities if it is still effectively to protect and promote its interests. In a dangerous world in which democracy is challenged by the rise of China, the revanchism of Russia, the barbarity of ISIS, the chaos of North Africa and the continuing problems of reforming Europe's economies, burying British heads in nostalgic sand is not an option. Britain must mine its long and distinguished tradition of exercising power in Europe to animate a new patriotism which gives hardened sceptics a reason to hope that a strong British continental policy need not be seen as treachery.

The aim of this book is to propose a policy which enables Britain to shine, not skulk, in Europe and play a more dynamic role on the world stage. It forsees a future where Britain is leading Europe with her allies and thereby in the world. To confront anew the three key issues of strengthening our security, improving our prosperity and promoting our common values, Britain will require a fresh start.

The fresh start will blend the UK's hard commercial and military power with its soft diplomatic and cultural power. The coercive or 'hard power' use of military resources will be increasingly important. But new and more subtle use of both 'hard' and 'soft' power is now vital for national effectiveness and advancement on the European and global stage. This is called 'smart power'.[3] Thus the fresh start Britain needs is hard power plus soft power equalling smart power – the use of both traditional and modern instruments of power to project and gain influence in a continent under threat.

Smart power requires a vision. But Acheson's remark has troubled the minds of all prime ministers and, in their own ways, they have tried and failed to entrench an enduring role either in the policies of their ministers or the minds of their people. With no understood policy anchor, British foreign policy since the war has bounced between leading and snubbing the Commonwealth, loving and hating Europe, scorning and cringing to the US.

While the US is the UK's close ally, and while the UK is a European power by history, geography and interests, leaders have never maximised the real influence gains for their country. The result is a public angry or indifferent about the future of their country. To avoid this 'victim syndrome' getting worse, Britain must now get back to a proper sense of itself, its role in Europe and the wider world.

So, first find your vision. The UK must articulate how the very most can be made of our undoubtedly unique assets and for what reason. The British need to know that the UK can be active without being ad hoc. The good news is that script is already in place.

Britain can dig into the past in order to find a path for the future. An unseen thread of smart power runs from Pitt the Younger, who inspired the Concert of Europe, through to the modern day. Disraeli, Gladstone and Joseph Chamberlain created a moral vision of a greater Britain, the heart of the three interlocking circles of Europe, the British Empire and the United States. In the 1940s Winston Churchill refreshed and renewed the vision, advocating a global Britain, at the heart of three interlocking circles of Europe, the Commonwealth and the United States.

In this book, we look at how this vision went unrealised by subsequent British leaders, how it can be revived as the basis for a new approach to Britain's place in the world and how it can be deployed in smart-power ways to increase British influence.

The problem is that Britain is weakening rather than bolstering its league position. Brexit aside, the UK's traditional rivals are enhancing their smart power on every front, including strengthening their cultural diplomacy institutions. China, Russia and other nations are also investing vast sums in supporting their strategies of power and influence assertion. For example, China has opened 327 of a projected 1,000 Confucius Institutes, encouraging philosophical understanding of its civilisation. India's investment in Bollywood has enlarged that country's cultural influence. Twenty-five countries have launched English-speaking world affairs news outlets while Britain has cut funding to the BBC World Service, closing 22 bureaus (including Ukraine) since 2011.

With many of the assets that pushed Britain to the top of the smart-power table now in play, Britain's soft power is threatened by competitors and its hard power atrophies after distant wars and defence cuts.

So the issue for this and future governments is whether they can renew Britain's world position, not as a bridge between Europe and the US, but as the synthesis of Churchill's three circles. Taking a more realistic view of the special relationship, a more active role in the commonwealth and a more strategic view of Europe would enhance British power.

Such ideas are nothing new. But to stay at the top of the global premier league, the UK must regain its sense of purpose to feel confident of its role in a transformed Europe and a turbulent world. And yet in the awkward affair with Europe, is Britain still going to act as the Mr Darcy of the continent, ignoring our neighbours' flirtations with a little pride and a lot of prejudice?

The aim of this book is to see how we got to this watershed moment and how Britain can avoid an historic relegation from power. How did we get here and how can we be smarter?

1

Pride

Churchill's Vision

... in which Churchill, following victory in the war, charts a new course to keep Britain great as a global leader at the centre of three circles – Europe, America and the Commonwealth – only to see the Europeans unite together without Britain, American power grow despite Britain and the Commonwealth's value ignored by Britain.

> We persist in regarding ourselves as a Great Power capable of everything and only temporarily handicapped by economic difficulties. We are not a Great Power and never will be again. We are a great nation, but if we continue to behave like a Great Power we shall soon cease to be a great nation.
>
> (Sir Henry Tizard, Chief Scientific Adviser to the Ministry of Defence, 1949)[1]

> For the makers of the original Europe their creation was a triumph. Out of defeat they produced a new kind of victory. For Britain, the entry into Europe was a defeat, a fate she had resisted, a necessity reluctantly accepted, the last resort of a once great power, never for one moment a climactic or triumphant engagement with the construction of Europe.
>
> (Hugo Young)[2]

Allies and influence: Churchill's three circles

It perhaps all begins in 1940, the hinge year, the finest hour. The frontier of democracy stands at Dover. Churchill's prose pounds the drumbeat of the British spirit urging the island people to fight on for freedom against near impossible odds.

Five years later, the armies of Britain, her empire and the United States had planted their flags of democracy, freedom and the rule of law in Berlin. it was a triumph of a vision. Harold Macmillan confessed to tears of pride when he saluted the victorious 8th Army and thought that, following victory, Britain's greatest era was about to unfold.

Neither Macmillan, nor his friend and chief, Churchill, were complacent about the future. Having won the war, they now would win the peace. For years they, together with Attlee, Bevin and the coalition, had debated how to maintain British power in a world of superpowers. Churchill conceived of an idea. It is as relevant today as it was then.

He drew three overlapping circles, with the UK in the centre. Here were the levers of Britain's future power. To serve the over-riding aim of keeping Britons living freely, prosperously and at peace, power would be exercised in future with the United States, the Commonwealth and Europe. He said:

> Now if you think of the three inter-linked circles you will see that we are the only country which has a great part in every one of them. We stand, in fact, at the very point of junction, and here in this Island at the centre of the seaways and perhaps of the airways also, we have the opportunity of joining them all together. If we rise to the occasion in the years that are to come it may be found that once again we hold the key to opening a safe and happy future to humanity, and will gain for ourselves gratitude and fame.[3]

These were not just honeyed words. Over the next five years this vision of a peaceful finest hour took shape. First, at the core of the new approach, Britain would partner the United States to deter Soviet aggression in Europe and elsewhere. Second, Britain, after Indian independence, would provide peripheral support by leading a new Commonwealth mission based on her residual strategic positions in the Middle East and Africa. Third, Britain would use her commanding position on the frontline in Europe to nurture a united, democratic continent. Bringing these threads together would underpin Churchill's vision of what he called 'world government' – a system in which law, not war, would govern disputes between states, and Britain would sit, with her allies, as a global umpire.

Before Churchill returned to power in 1951, each of his circles was in place under a Labour government within the new world order. His former Labour colleagues in the wartime coalition did the hard graft. The diplomacy of Attlee's foreign secretary, Ernest Bevin, revolved around the continuation of the Commonwealth and the view that Britain must remain a Great Power. Bevin crafted a new 'Third Force' Commonwealth endorsed by the US in 1948. In 1949 the NATO treaty was signed, entrenching the American alliance as the bulwark against communism. In the same year, Churchill's Council of Europe was founded.

All seemed set fair. As the new post-imperial era began, Britain's statesmen had the chance to create more modern and sustainable foundations for the UK's world position. But what follows is the story of a great man's ambition foiled and British power squandered. Macmillan's tears on that victorious podium hid the saddest delusion – shared by him, the establishment and the 45 million islanders. Britain was going to lose her empire and fail to find a role. It needn't have been this way. It is a crisis we are still living with.

Narrower still and narrower: The British dilemma

Victory was like a drug. At the end of World War II the Empire still stood. A new Elizabethan age was soon to dawn. At that time there was simply no desire or need to rush into entangling alliances when Britain bestrode the world. There were still plates to spin and there was no need to drop any. By 1945, with the sun still shining on the Union flag and the Navy ruling the waves, the Empire wrapped the British people in a psychological mink coat which they were very reluctant to shake off.

So began Britain's postwar 70 years of juggling Churchill's three circles, in the form of the United States, European partners and the Commonwealth. Nineteen general elections, nine changes of governing party, six major economic crises, one lost empire, and still, as Oliver Franks pointed out, 'it is part of the habit and furniture of our minds to be a Great Power. Britain must be at as many top tables at which we can find a seat'.[4] Why?

At the heart of this story is how Britain created the myth of its place in the world and sold it to the British people. Global influence became a British tradition. In 1872, at the Crystal Palace, Benjamin Disraeli said that the purpose of any governing party was to maintain the nation's institutions, uphold the Empire and elevate the condition of the people.[5] Disraeli was the first Victorian politician to see that a robust world role could glue the nation together. It became the basis for what it meant to be British. Expansion in India and Africa forged a new consciousness of what it was to be patriotic. It enabled national leaders to portray their opponents as little Englanders, hostile to Britain's Empire-fuelled world hegemony.

The Empire was seen as a natural extension of the institutions that forged modern Britain. By the 1880s it was the British way that dominated the financial, political and commercial world networks, in the same way as the United States did after 1945. It was all a seamless story. Disraeli had inaugurated a period of 'prestige politics'[6] in which a new British myth would emerge to defend the 1688 Glorious Revolution and the 1707 Union with Scotland. The sovereignty of the Crown in Parliament, the Englishness of the established Church, the Royal Navy and the law were the beating heart of the successful British state. Maintaining the state required order, hierarchy and authority.

It was a simple philosophy that blended faith in the trusted institutions of the British state at home with pride in the success of the British state abroad. The establishment were clever enough to employ flexibility in massaging the forces that, from time to time, opposed this settlement. The twin loyalties to country and Empire coursed through the veins of the body politic. They provided a political elixir: a ready-made identity, a narrative for Britain.

But it was not until Joseph Chamberlain emerged as the first neo-con in the 1890s that the Empire became a policy cornerstone. Successful aggrandisement in South Africa in the Boer War was followed by the feeling that the Empire could expand no further. Instead of wider and wider, Chamberlain wanted it deeper and deeper. He wanted 'imperial preference' – a protective tariff wall around a quarter of the globe to pay for Disraeli's policy of elevating the condition of the people. He wanted an Imperial Parliament, bringing the dominions together at Westminster, to demonstrate British might. He judged that to maintain supremacy the Empire must become a self-financing fortress with a global reach.

Yet Chamberlain was no splendid isolationist. In his ambitions for British influence he conceived of the parallel idea of bringing Germany and the United States into a global alliance with the British Empire. This was the foundation stone of Churchill's three circles.

It is difficult today to envision how globally successful Chamberlain's empire was. As a political idea, it attractively linked a domestic social reform agenda with the continuance of Britain's power. It brought the classes together in a One Nation mix of domestic and foreign policy that was Disraeli's brainchild. As a policy it led in 1925 to the foreign secretary, Sir Austen Chamberlain, sealing British leadership in Europe by concluding the Locarno Pact. And in 1932 it sealed British leadership in the Empire when Chancellor Neville Chamberlain signed imperial preference into law with the Ottawa Accords. This was a family business. But it was Neville Chamberlain who would end his father's idea of empire shortly after its high-water mark. Hitler overturned Locarno. Gandhi blunted the Empire and the Depression soured the link between welfare and the flag.[7]

The price of European appeasement and imperial weakness meant the growing power of the United States needed harnessing to bolster the Empire. Churchill saw this clearly. Already cooperation with the United States had brought the 1921 Washington Naval Treaty which ended the two-power standard and granted the US parity with the Royal Navy. But this was a Faustian bargain. Churchill knew that the United States wanted an end to imperial preference which denied access to American goods. Others wanted an end to the Empire itself as an offence against democracy and a barrier to American power.

But Churchill's Herculean task of winning the war by joining with the United States and mobilising the Empire to liberate Europe meant that these anxieties seemed tolerable compared to surrendering to Hitler. In preventing Hitler from conquering Britain, Churchill ensured that Nazi Germany would not win the war. He could not, however, defeat Hitler without the aid of the United States. And yet Lend-Lease and the 1942 Atlantic Charter alerted Churchill to troubles ahead, reflecting that it would be 'easier … to forgive our present enemies in their future misery, starvation and weakness than to reconcile ourselves to the past claims and future demands of our allies'.[8]

Churchill had realised during the war that Britain's power was crumbling. 'There I sat,' he said of the Tehran conference in 1943,

> with the great Russian bear on one side of me, with paws outstretched, and on the other side the great American buffalo, and between the two sat the poor little English donkey who was the only one who knew the right way home.[9]

But in 1945 with Hitler dead and the United States dominant, the real question was how to ensure that Britain's global role would not be killed by the kindness of friends, rather than the brutality of continental enemies.

Churchill was faced with three options to keep Britain's head held high:

> It could try to lead a united Europe as a force in world politics; it could develop the Commonwealth as an alternative power bloc, a course often favoured by the Labour left; or it could revive the wartime Anglo-American alliance to stand against Russia.[10]

As these alternatives were not mutually exclusive, the only question was how they could be united. Perhaps there was a new role for the three circles of Chamberlain's empire which Churchill could forge?

Forging the three circles: The road to Suez

Churchill hoped to restore British power in the same way that he had defied Hitler, by matching this grand vision with a supreme act of political will. He knew he had to reconcile the competing demands of Europe, the Commonwealth and the United States. He had sketched his vision of three circles of influence during the war. Now he had to announce it to the British people, which he did in October 1948 at the Conservative conference at Llandudno.

Churchill made clear that Britain held a unique position at the heart of 'three majestic circles': the 'Empire and Commonwealth', 'the English-speaking world' and a 'United Europe'. Churchill described these three circles as 'co-existent' and 'linked together'.

In Churchill's vision, the nation's external action had to be dictated by a consideration of the power Britain could exert through, firstly, bilateral relationships with the United States; secondly, its involvement in formal and informal networks of influence with the Commonwealth; and thirdly by rebuilding Europe.

Britain must stand on terms of near-equality with the United States precisely because, as Churchill told the French foreign minister in 1949, 'Britain cannot be thought of as a single state in isolation. She is the founder and centre of a world-wide Empire and Commonwealth.'[11] Adding British leadership in Europe to the power balance, he believed, would enable him to look the United States square in the eyes.

With the policy set, but vague enough to be open to interpretation, what followed was an agonising struggle to link the circles together. Success in this endeavour would provide the UK with a credible postwar grand strategy. Britain would act with the French as a co-leader in Europe, with the Commonwealth as a co-leader in the wider world and with the Americans as a co-leader in the Cold War. This would require the UK to devise a clear narrative for itself over the long term: to be a regional, cultural and global power. Failure to do so would lead to retreat, confusion and missed opportunities in all three historic theatres.

The next ten years would demonstrate Britain's tragic inability to spin three plates at the same time. In Europe, what began with the liberated nations urging Churchill and Bevin to assume continental leadership stalled into a process of more reluctant engagement ending with two failed applications to join the EEC. Relations with the United States, which began with the UK, despite its economic problems, seeking and getting United States support for Britain leading in NATO, Europe and the Commonwealth, ended with a long identity crisis in which Britain went from partner to supplicant, a loss of grandeur seared in the humiliation of the 1956 Suez Crisis. The chance of establishing a new hegemony in the Middle East and Africa was missed, as the post-Suez 'Winds of Change' decolonisation robbed Britain of what little Commonwealth authority could have been salvaged from the wreck of Empire.

The oscillation of the overlapping circles showed Britain being buffeted by events and forced into difficult choices rather than implementing a sustainable grand strategy. Without clear policy direction in these early years, Churchill's three circles defaulted to prioritise the United States and the dying Commonwealth over and above Europe.

The reasons soon became obvious. Failure to hold the circles steady was down to three foreign secretaries: Ernest Bevin,

Anthony Eden and Harold Macmillan. The first was dead by 1951 and the other two each became prime minister. It was the clash of their dreams – between themselves and with events – that dashed the chance of fulfilling Churchill's plan. It was a failure of smart power. What went wrong?

From the Commonwealth circle to Suez

Looking at it now, resisting the collapse of British imperial power – all but complete by the mid-1960s – seems an ignorant and stubborn move by the British establishment. The end can be traced directly to the impact of World War II. The catastrophic British defeats in Europe and Asia between 1940 and 1942 destroyed Britain's financial and economic independence, the real foundation of the imperial system. Britain had certainly survived the war, but its wealth, prestige and authority had been severely reduced. The war also erased the old balance of power on which British security – at home and abroad – had largely depended. Although Britain was one of the victorious Allies, the defeat of Germany had been mainly the work of Soviet and American power, while that of Japan had been an almost entirely American triumph.

But this was not the way Anthony Eden's Foreign Office saw it at the time. Following a number of studies conducted in 1944, they reached a different conclusion. The primary objective of state planners following World War II was to preserve Britain's role and global status as a Great Power and to do so they concluded that Britain should restore its pre-war Chamberlainite focus on Empire after 1945.

And yet by doing so the British found themselves locked into an imperial endgame. An early symptom of the weakness of the Empire was Britain's withdrawal from India in 1947. Britain hoped that a self-governing India would remain part of the postwar imperial defence network. For this reason, Britain was desperate to keep India (and its army) united. These hopes came to nothing. The last viceroy, Lord Louis Mountbatten, realising that unless he agreed to partition, chaos and religious war would break out, devised a swift handover to two successor governments (India and Pakistan) before the ink was dry on their post-imperial frontiers.

The quiet satisfaction at the relatively courtly departure disguised the fact that the end of the Raj was a bitter blow to British world power. Britain had lost the colony that had provided much of its military muscle east of Suez, as well as paying 'rent' for the 'hire' of much of Britain's own army. The burden of Empire defence shifted back to a Britain that was both weaker and poorer than it had been before 1939. And that economic weakness in the early postwar period undermined any hope of restoring Chamberlain's empire. The war cost £7.3 billion, a quarter of Britain's pre-war wealth, and left Britain with £3.3 billion worth of debt. If the future of Britain was to be at the centre of anything, the restoration of the pre-war order had to be abandoned. Soon, Ernest Bevin conjured up a more balanced and imaginative approach, represented by Churchill's three circles.

The Third Force

The loss of India led to a drastic reappraisal of Britain's world interests. Britain was now overshadowed by two new superpowers, the United States and the Soviet Union. British prime minister Clement Attlee and his Cabinet colleague Ernest Bevin, who dominated Labour's foreign policy at the time, drew quite radical conclusions with regard to the future of Britain's overseas interests.

In January and March 1948 Bevin circulated four memos to the Labour Cabinet. The 'Third Force' memos diagnosed the threat posed to democracies by totalitarian Stalinism and outlined a distinctive social democratic response. He strongly asserted Britain's status as a Great Power, cherishing ideas that Britain's power-base could be, not India, but the 'middle of the planet' independent of both the US and the USSR. Bevin believed the US should support this policy. In his view, Britain's sacrifices in the common cause justified the US providing financial help to, in effect, underwrite Britain's new empire without undermining it.

Attlee and Bevin's plan was sound. They sent Field Marshal Montgomery to Africa to plan how to exploit the tropical colonies more effectively so that their cocoa, rubber and tin could be sold for much-needed dollars.[12] Nor was the imperative behind this idea simply economic. Britain's strategic defence against the new Soviet threat required forward air bases from which to bomb southern Russia – the industrial arsenal of the Soviet Union. That meant staying on in the Middle East even after the breakdown of British control in Palestine and its hasty evacuation in 1948.

In Egypt, Iraq, Jordan and the Gulf, the British were determined to hang on to their treaties and bases, including the vast Suez Canal zone. They wanted help from Australia and hoped for Indian support against Soviet influence in Asia. Across the whole spectrum of party opinion, British leaders had no doubt that Britain must uphold its status as the third Great Power, and that it could do so, first and foremost, by creating new Commonwealth power centres in Africa and the Middle East.

They also believed Britain's economic recovery and the survival of sterling as a great trading currency required closer integration with the old 'white' dominions, especially Australia, New Zealand and South Africa. The 'sterling area', which included the Commonwealth (the main exception was Canada) and some other countries, accounted for half of the world's trade in the early postwar years.

To deliver this new policy, even a propaganda unit, the Information Research Department, was established to promote a 'Future Foreign Publicity Policy'. But during the next two years the department's positive, Third Force mission became eclipsed by a more negative anti-communist message. The escalation of the Cold War in Europe, the increasing economic weakness of Britain and, finally, the outbreak of the Korean War in 1950 all combined to make Bevin realise that promoting the Commonwealth circle through the Third Force could not be done without working more closely with Europe and the United States. He knew cooperation was the only means of securing Britain's status as a Great Power.

From the European circle to Suez

The plan was to link the Commonwealth to a European 'Western Union'. Although he had Churchill's Council of Europe as a foundation for a new British approach to the continent, Bevin would not be the first statesman to confront the reality that it is to the benefit, confusion and misfortune of the UK that the country was forged in opposition to Europe.

With 1.3 million Britons dead on Europe's battlefields in a generation and less than ten years since the Battle of Britain, selling union with former enemies would never be easy. Since Britain emerged as a nation state in opposition to Rome in 1534, it had fought the Catholicism of Spain, the mercantilism of Holland, the revolution of France and the imperialism of Germany.

Often forgotten was that, between these defiant moments of 1588, 1784, 1815, 1918 and 1940, Britain acted as the leader of Europe. Moreover, a leader with a clear political purpose – to stop dominance by one nation in Europe and to promote the perennial values of freedom, democracy and the rule of law. For 500 years, successive British leaders argued for liberal interventionism in Europe. The objectives were clear and so were the methods: divide and rule, not splendid isolation. As William Pitt the Younger said in 1805, 'England has saved herself by her exertions, and will, as I trust, save Europe by her example.'[13]

But creating and financing coalitions of the willing was a very different thing to the new Europe that would emerge when Britain, in the absence of a clear British policy, chose not to lead by example. From the 1950s to the present day, it was not engagement with Europe that was the problem but the challenge of facing what was viewed as a new supranational threat to Parliament's power.

Postwar British policy towards Europe can only be understood as a clash between the pre-war Westphalian order, where, since the 1648 treaty which ended the Thirty Years War, state power was absolute, and the postwar world order, where it was not.

So began the five stages over 50 years during which Churchill's European circle emerged from theory into practice:

(1) Indifference to 1961: Britain looked askance and from afar at the creation of the European Coal and Steel Community and declined to participate in the Messina negotiations which led to the Treaty of Rome.

(2) Interest to 1975: Britain, marooned after Suez, began a series of applications to join the European Economic Community (EEC), only to have the mirror of rejection turned to it by de Gaulle, who had felt rejected himself from the postwar top tables, and who rejected Britain's Commonwealth and Anglo-American preferences despite the fact that they yielded little at that time in hard power. Admission in 1973 and the referendum that confirmed membership seemed to lay the matter to rest.

(3) Importance to 1990: During the sclerotic 1970s, when the nine EEC member states grappled with external crises, Britain's engagement was limited. However, British inspiration created the most significant forward policy in Europe's history to date: the 1992 programme establishing the Single Market.

(4) Irritation to 2009: The 20 years that straddled the millennium represented the high water mark in the battle of ideas between the federalists and the British. The score was 1–1. The British championed the enlargement of the EU. The federalists championed the euro and the constitution. Enlargement was a signal success. The euro teeters towards failure. The constitution was a disaster.

(5) Reckoning from 2010: With a Conservative-led and, after 2015, purely Conservative government, the long story of British discomfort with this phase of European cooperation reached its conclusion in the vote to leave the EU and seek a new relationship with Europe.

However, it started well. Between 1945 and 1948 Britain was enthusiastic about taking European leadership. Then, between 1949 and 1960 it tried to guide the process in an intergovernmental direction, in an attempt to appease Eden and the imperialists and to contain the supranational ambitions of the six founding members of the European Economic Community.

Bevin, 1945–1950

The European policy pursued by the Foreign Office between 1945 and 1948 envisaged the creation of some form of European entity led by Britain. For Bevin, British foreign policy was now to be constructed around 'three main pillars ... the Commonwealth, Western Europe, and the United States.'[14] Bevin had recognised the need for a defensive political 'Western bloc' of European countries, but he knew that this must be supported by a single, self-supporting economic unit pooling the resources of its members with Britain at its heart.

The idea was to regenerate the continent and preserve a lasting peace in Europe, in part to counter the strained relations between Britain, the Soviet Union and the United States. So the 1947 Treaty of Dunkirk between Britain and France was the first step in a future 'Western Union' linked to Bevin's 'Third Force' that would dominate between Northern Europe and Southern Africa. And the 1949 Treaty of London, which created the Council of Europe, was the first step in entrenching a new political order guaranteeing democracy, human rights and freedom.

In his 1948 New Year radio broadcast, Attlee said:

> It is for us, as Europeans, and not the Americans, to give the lead in (the) spiritual, moral and political sphere to all the democratic elements in Western Europe and, at the same time, genuinely progressive and reformist, believing in freedom and social justice – what one might call the 'Third Force' ... We should advertise our principles as offering the best and most efficient way of life.

Bevin reiterated this, saying: 'We should do all we can to foster both the spirit and the machinery of cooperation ... Britain cannot stand outside Europe and regard her problems as quite separate from those of her European neighbours.'

So in early January 1948, Bevin presented to the Cabinet a memorandum, 'The First Aim of British Foreign Policy', stating that:

> It is not enough to reinforce the physical barriers which still guard our western civilisation. We must organise and consolidate the ethical and spiritual forces inherent in this western civilisation of which we are the chief protagonists. This in my view can only be done by creating some form of union in Western Europe, whether of a formal or informal character, backed by the Americas and the Dominions. The countries of Western Europe ... will look to us for political and moral guidance.[15]

Bevin's intention, therefore, was to create a base in Europe and Africa which would allow Britain to act as a superpower in a 'partnership between equals' with the US. Far from antagonising the United States, this approach was popular in the US State Department, where policy makers wanted to create a confident, strong Western Europe independent of US support.

But it was not long before Britain's financial instability encouraged Bevin to extend his 'bloc' to incorporate the US within it in order to bolster the defence of Western Europe, a task that Britain could not adequately fulfil. The three circles were to be forged not only through Churchillian vision and geopolitical opportunity but to pay the bills.

Four schemes were combined: Anglo-French economic coordination in a European customs union, political cooperation through the Council of Europe, a 'Euro-Africa' plan based on the common exploitation of Anglo-French colonies and United States military and economic help. Bevin stated:

> provided we can organise a Western European system such as I have outlined above, backed by the power and resources of the Commonwealth and of the Americas, it should be possible to develop our own power and influence to equal that of the United States of America. We have the material resources in the Colonial Empire, if we develop them, and by giving a

> spiritual lead now we should be able to carry out our task in a way which will show clearly that we are not subservient to the United States of America.

Despite the recognition of his dependency on American financial and military power, and yet backed strongly by them, Bevin's interventions show British determination to seize a leadership role in Europe.

But, in the first of many setbacks to this dream, by late 1950 Bevin's energy was fading through ill health and he was soon dead at the age of 70. The Korean War focused the minds of policy makers on the enormity of the communist threat in the East, as the gradual Soviet takeover of Eastern Europe did in the West. Suddenly, European and Commonwealth *grands projets* looked like an unaffordable luxury.

Recalling Bevin's leadership, Paul-Henri Spaak, the Belgian prime minister and first chairman of the Organisation for European Economic Co-operation's Council, said that 'never again was he to show up in that early light. On the contrary, he seemed surprised and even worried when he saw the ideas, which he himself had pioneered, being put into practice'.[16] Spaak 'never understood why Bevin changed his view as he did'.

Eden, 1951–1955

The reason was that by 1950, on both economic and security fronts, the Foreign Office felt that ensuring a strong relationship with the United States was the only game in town and the only immediate way of retaining global importance. Also, the Schuman Declaration of 9 May 1950 laid out a plan for a European Community that would pool the coal and steel of its members in a common market, a proposal too minor and complex to interest the British. Europe was too complicated, poor and remote.

In an interdepartmental meeting of Foreign Office, Treasury and other officials they outlined the essential characteristics of the policy, which operated under the new foreign secretary, Anthony Eden:

> Our policy should be to assist Europe to recover as far as we can. But the concept must be one of limited liability. In no

> circumstances must we assist them beyond the point at which the assistance leaves us too weak to be a worthwhile ally for the US if Europe collapses, i.e. beyond the point at which our own viability was impaired. Nor can we embark upon measures of 'co-operation' which surrender our sovereignty and which lead us down paths along which there is no return.[17]

So, despite the clear opportunity open to Britain and the encouragement of the United States, Churchill's European circle – despite Bevin's success in establishing the institutions and the vision to build it – was sidelined in the belief that the global communist threat required a binary choice between leading in Europe and forging the Anglo-American 'special relationship'. Over the next three years, Britain's rejection of the Schuman Plan and its opposition to the European Defence Community and European Political Community encouraged early Euroscepticism. Anthony Eden's plan, published in February 1952,[18] was its founding document. In it he proposed that the supranational Schuman Plan and the European Defence Community would be subsumed into a reformed intergovernmental Council of Europe. Eden rejected Churchill-style European utopianism with a pragmatic opposition to the 'small group of states which are moving towards political federation by the progressive establishment of organisations exercising supranational powers'.[19]

This view was rejected by the Treasury. Before the 1955 Messina Conference which led to the Treaty of Rome, Treasury economists had concluded that the benefits of joining the EEC would exceed any loss of Commonwealth markets. But armed with the Eden Plan, the Foreign Office disagreed, warning that it would be 'a discriminatory bloc most unwelcome to us',[20] an approach which ended with the British attempt to wreck the Conference before it began.

Although the original six members of the EEC had invited Britain to join the negotiations without preconditions, by November 1955 Eden decided to withdraw. The UK had tried to persuade the continental powers to reduce import controls, let their currencies float and create a European free market. As a harbinger of battles over economic philosophy to come, Britain's proposals were rejected. The original six were keener on Bevin's customs union.

But the Foreign Office was now hostile to what had been its own policy, declaring that:

> Once we became members of a common market, we should be subject to strong political pressures to extend the 'harmonisation' of our policies with those of other members beyond the field of tariffs into other fields both of internal and external policy.

If a proposal for a common market of the 'Six' came into being, it would be so 'dangerous to our economic interests that we should have to make special arrangements with it, even at the expense of our interests elsewhere'.[21]

It seemed obvious to Eden that the defeated powers wanted an introverted protectionist bloc. In November 1955 the Foreign Office declared that Britain was not against special groupings of European member countries 'but we shall remain a bit sceptical and suspicious of the Monnets of the European world who, having failed so far in their special political objectives, are now using the slogan of "economic integration" as their stalking horse'.[22]

For the still imperially minded Whitehall and Westminster, washing British hands of what they believed to be a *sotto voce* anti-US micro-project was deemed entirely understandable. This was because after 1950 British policy was framed by hostility to pooling sovereignty with a social democratic Europe, excessive belief in the Commonwealth's power and confidence that the 'special relationship' was the geopolitical priority despite American support for the idea of British leadership on the continent. However, snubbed by Eden, the European founding fathers pressed on. Spaak concluded that 'we must do without Britain's support if we are to make any headway', adding with sadness:

> There is one thing you British will never understand: an idea. And there is one thing you are supremely good at grasping: a

> hard fact. We will have to make Europe without you but then you will have to come in and join us.

Spaak agreed with Jean Monnet that they should 'create Churchill's Europe and Britain will join'.[23]

From the American circle to Suez

So by 1955 far from further linking the two circles of Europe and America, the UK believed it more practical to keep them separate. On balance, economic cooperation with Europe came second to closer security cooperation with the United States. The question was, while the threat of Schuman's federal Europe eating British power dissuaded the British from linking to the European circle, could more influence be gained from the Commonwealth and American ones?

In the years 1946 to 1948, United States foreign policy was in a state of flux as the penny dropped that the Soviet Union was not going to be a partner but a rival. The relationship with Great Britain that had been forged during World War II developed uncertainly towards partnership in response to the new conditions of peace, increased American economic power, the development of national security ideas and the commitment to active participation in world affairs.

After a shaky start, with the reduction of military cooperation to a peacetime basis and the difficult negotiations over a loan from the US to Britain at the end of 1945, Churchill's plea at Fulton, Missouri, in 1946 for a renewed Anglo-American alliance was followed by the Truman Doctrine, Marshall Aid, and the breakdown of cooperation with the Soviet Union in 1947.

While this outcome was undoubtedly one of which Churchill approved, it should not be assumed that his and Bevin's views of the United States and its connection to the United Kingdom, and, most importantly, its attitude to British vital interests, were different.

The one-sided nature of the 'special relationship', a situation of British dependence rather than Anglo-American partnership, was acknowledged by Churchill and Bevin as early as August 1945.

Britain was a 'junior partner in an orbit of power predominantly under American aegis'.[24] The Foreign Office's 1947 assessment warned that 'too great an independence of the United States would be a dangerous luxury', while acknowledging that the US was 'consciously or unconsciously tending to claim global leadership'.[25]

However, the illusion of equality was deemed a price worth paying for Britain and Europe's economic survival. In February 1949 Bevin sanctioned the creation of the Permanent Under-Secretary's Committee, equivalent to the US State Department Policy Planning Staff, to consider long-term questions of foreign policy and to make recommendations. One such report, produced in March 1949, identified the centrality of Anglo-American relations to British policy. 'In the face of implacable Soviet hostility and in view of our economic dependence on the United States, the immediate problem is to define the nature of our relationship with the United States.'[26] Another report produced in March 1949 highlighted the 'importance of our maintaining control of the periphery' around the Soviet Union 'which runs round from Oslo to Tokyo'. It recommended that 'this policy should be concerted with the United States'.[27]

President Truman and Dean Acheson, his secretary of state, subscribed to this view. In 1950 they agreed with the importance of Britain's position at the intersection of Churchill's circles:

> There is no country on earth whose interests are so wrapped around the world as the UK ... She is in more vitally strategic areas than any other nation among the community of Western nations. She is the center of a great Commonwealth ... She is the center of the sterling area ... held together ... by an intricate and complicated system of commercial and financial arrangements built up tediously by the British ... There is no substitute for the sterling area and none can be erected in any short period of time. But beyond all these considerations the UK is the only power, in addition to ourselves, West of the Iron Curtain capable of wielding substantial military strength. This assembly of facts ... makes a special relationship between the US and the UK as inescapable as the facts themselves.[28]

It was an attractive narrative, not only because of the perceived fact that the English-speaking peoples had rescued the Old World from itself in 1945. Anglo-America was a powerful myth in its own right. It was a transnational political space which, no less than the Empire itself, was an imagined community bound together by a common language and history. So Chamberlain's concept seemed uniquely relevant again. Although it was apparent that, in purely economic terms, Britain was temporarily embarrassed and dependent on the United States, there was little doubt, in British eyes, that the Commonwealth could co-exist with the United States, dividing superpower responsibilities. The British were used to seeing themselves as a world island, pioneering new developments and creating models which others would copy and adapt. Why not now blend Britain's first empire, lost by Cornwallis at Yorktown in 1781, with its second empire to establish the Anglo-Saxon confederation, the Greater Britain never consummated?

So the main significance of Anglo-America for the future of British politics lay in its powerful story as a global hegemon. It was felt to be a praetorian guard governing the world economy and managing the international state system and in particular the rules and conditions for an open liberal world order. It is little wonder that Anglo-America came to represent for Britain an alternative to involvement in Europe, as a means of preserving its long-standing ideal of an open free-trade liberal order.

But internal contradictions were always likely to destroy Eden's fanciful hopes of creating a Chamberlainite Anglo-American imperium:

- The United States was deeply suspicious of the Commonwealth's fundamental lack of democracy.
- The United States was determined to destroy imperial preference in the name of global free trade.
- The United Kingdom played an increasingly second-fiddle role to the United States and was unable to sustain its power pretence.

- The United States wanted the United Kingdom to play a full part in the unification of Europe.

It didn't take long for the hubristic reality check to come, sooner than expected, in 1956.

Decline and fall: Suez, 1956

History often brings all political strands together in one defining incident. Sometimes with individuals, sometimes with unexpected events. Most spectacularly both. The Suez Crisis of 1956 unlinked the three circles. The Anglo-French expedition to retake the canal was effectively derailed by the United States. It ended at once British strategic freedom of action, its power in the Middle East and the *entente cordiale* as an instrument of European military authority. It ended Anglo-French cooperation aimed at creating a Western Union in Europe. It ended the Third Force unity of the Commonwealth. And it ended the illusion of Anglo-American co-leadership. Urged by the anti-imperial State Department, President Eisenhower finally pulled the financial rug from underneath the British. The lion's roar was silenced by Britain's friends, not its enemies.

The British and French famously drew different conclusions from Suez and thereby gave up on the prospect of effective cooperative action between the two most global European powers. The fact was that the French were more agile in re-orienting their foreign policy with regard to Europe. France determined to construct Europe in its own image before Britain was in a position to put spokes in the Gallic wheel. Had Suez erupted before the Messina negotiations, it is conceivable that the existential dust could have settled to enable the British Government to see the future more clearly. But it didn't.

The Suez crisis fall-out precipitated a shift in policy as Britain went back to the drawing board. Was there any conceivable way of reviving the three circles? Unpalatable facts were faced by the Conservative establishment. By 1956 Britain's choice to trade in the leadership of Europe in order to bind the Commonwealth into the American circle meant that of Churchill's three circles one had been abandoned and the other two fused together. For that reason, Britain shunned the negotiations which led to the European Coal and Steel Community and stood on the sidelines in 1955 at Messina at the conference which led to the Treaty of Rome.

It became clear that the Eden Plan – putting all eggs in the Commonwealth and American baskets to the exclusion of Europe – had been unwise. An application to join the EEC meant that Britain could try to have the best of all worlds. It could add ballast to its declining international clout by returning to the European stage in order to exercise more leverage over the United States.

This was completely understood by the Americans. Assessing Britain's role post-Suez, George Ball, Under-Secretary of State for Economic Affairs, set out why the US supported British entry:

> If Britain is now prepared to recognise that the Rome Treaty is not a static document but a process that could eventually lead to an evolving European Community, something in the nature of a European federation, and if Britain can make the great national decision to join Europe on these terms, I am confident that my government will regard this as a major contribution to Western solidarity and the stability of the free world.[29]

End of the three circles?

Despite the now received view that all British governments were pro-European before the advent of Margaret Thatcher, Britain in fact failed to rise to the Churchillian vision that its destiny was as a moral leader at the centre of the three circles of global influence. Lip service was paid to the policy, but the challenges were too great. First, the timing was wrong. It is true that had Britain seized European leadership after 1945, the continent could have developed in a more intergovernmental manner based more on Churchill's Council of Europe model than the Schuman model. Second, it is also true that a Bevinite 'Third Force' empire was possible, with French and American support, that would have dominated the Middle East and Africa, shoring up oil and precious mineral resources. Third, it is also true that a special relationship with the United States could have been based not only on the geopolitical importance of NATO against the Soviet Union, but on UK leadership in the European, African and Middle East spheres of influence.

But imagination dies hard. The British Empire had won the war against Germany and Japan. Britain had her finest hour as a moral redoubt against European chaos. The United States would lead the global fight in the Cold War to come with Britain at her side. The American and Commonwealth sentimental, security and commercial alliance was imprinted still in the minds and the balance sheets of the British establishment.

Had Bevin succeeded in gaining acceptance for his new narrative for the Commonwealth after Indian independence in 1947 based on Middle Eastern and African power, had Churchill shaped early European integration based on his Council of Europe concept and had Eden practised better diplomacy with Eisenhower, the three circles would have had a better chance of linking. Instead only the special relationship became a permanent, if unequal, association. The Commonwealth withered. And Europe remained a question unanswered.

2

Prejudice

From Macmillan to Cameron

... in which Britain's leaders try to revive Churchill's three circles in order to reestablish Britain as a global leader, only to see the Europeans unite together to prevent a resurgent Germany, America seek more European integration and the Commonwealth's value reduced to rubble.

> It is a matter of profound regret to me that much political energy ... is still devoted to the hoary question of whether we should be in or out. We must not allow ourselves to be deflected into an arid debate about the past and away from our purpose, which is to build a strong and enduring Community and to improve Britain's position within it. The unity of Europe as a force for peace, freedom and democracy is a goal for which I pledge to work.
>
> (Margaret Thatcher, London, 1983)

> Our destiny is in Europe, as part of the Community. That is not to say that our future lies only in Europe.
>
> (Margaret Thatcher, Bruges, 1988)

> I am such a passionate believer in the Community that I accept the accusation of being a troublemaker. But I am not awkward; I just want Europe to work.
>
> (Margaret Thatcher, 1990)

Forgetting the three circles: The road to 'In'

Macmillan, 1957–1961

When the Treaty of Rome established the EEC, the *Financial Times* entitled its editorial column on 25 March 1957 the 'End of the Beginning'. Borrowing the phrase from Winston Churchill, it predicted that the Treaty marked only the start of a process of economic change: 'There is no doubt that the structure of European industry will be very different by 1970 from what it would be without the Common Market scheme.' Britain's place in the new calculus of Europe was worthy of mention only in so far as it was assumed to be an interested bystander.

Only four months after the Suez debacle, what was striking was the absence of any concern that Britain was now adrift. Though Europe was the primary Foreign Office bugbear under Eden, missing from the article was an appreciation of the political ambitions of the founding fathers as they sought a new political concert between the peoples of the continent. For the British, the Common Market was still a trading bloc and one with anti-Commonwealth and anti-US leanings as well. Here in the combination of arrogant disdain and strategic miscalculation lay the error that explains Britain's troubled relationship with its European neighbours. British policy subsequently failed to escape the misjudgement, implicit in that *Financial Times* editorial, that despite Bevin's leadership and imagination, Europe was always an afterthought for the establishment.

However, from 1957 a new generation of officials joined the civil service, displacing those loyal to Eden's now discredited imperialism. This inspired the development of a new pro-entry orthodoxy within the Foreign Office and the Treasury which 'amounted to a revolution in political thought; in a short period at the beginning of the sixties entry to the EU was turned from an impossibility into an imperative'.[1] The rationale behind this new orthodoxy was that the Foreign Office came round to seeing Europe as 'an empire on our doorstep', while the Treasury believed that 'if Britain could acquire an expanded home market, then industrial revival would follow'.[2]

In March 1960 an interdepartmental committee of senior civil servants, chaired by Sir Frank Lee, was established to review Britain's European policy. The Lee memorandum argued that negotiating entry would involve 'difficult and unpalatable decisions', including, as Churchill had acknowledged, the surrender of some sovereignty. It recommended a policy of 'near identification', that is, accepting many of its obligations without formal membership. Harold Macmillan, Eden's successor as prime minister, subsequently stated that the 'policies of "near identification"' and of joining the Common Market were so similar that one might well lead to the other, and if we were prepared to accept near identification, it might be preferable to contemplate full membership.[3] He realised that the EEC had 'brought France, Germany, and the United States closer together on a range of economic issues and further alienated Britain'.[4]

In June 1960 Macmillan circulated a memorandum to officials, asking them to answer 23 questions. The subsequent report, discussed by a Cabinet committee, stated that:

> We cannot join the Common Market on the cheap. First we must accept that there will have to be a political content in our action – we must show ourselves prepared to join with the Six in their institutional arrangements and in any development towards closer political integration. Without this we cannot achieve our foreign policy aims. Secondly, there must be a real intention to have a 'common market'. In general we must accept the common tariff.[5]

The Cabinet discussed the Lee memorandum in July 1960. However, it was apparent that it was divided on the benefits and costs of entry. Two weeks later, Macmillan reshuffled the Cabinet in favour of pro-membership ministers. Because he feared navigating a Conservative Party confused by Suez and dismayed by imperial retreat, Macmillan's new European policy, in effect a decision to join the EEC, was made by civil servants. Sir Roy Denman, the Cabinet Office coordinator for European affairs, claimed that 'it must be the only occasion in British history when a memorandum by an official was largely responsible for a momentous change in British foreign policy'.[6]

In March 1961 George Ball re-emphasised US support for British entry. In a meeting with Edward Heath and Sir Frank Lee, Ball stated that 'the United States deeply regretted that the United Kingdom had not yet felt able to accept the Rome Treaty commitments. British membership of the Community would represent a contribution of great importance to the cohesion of the Free World.'[7]

Between April and July 1961 several Cabinet committee meetings discussed the implications of entry. The Lord Chancellor, Lord Kilmuir, assessed the legal implications, warning that:

- Parliament would be required to surrender some of its functions to the organs of the Community.
- The Crown would be called on to transfer part of its treaty-making power to those organs.
- Our courts of law would sacrifice some degree of independence by becoming subordinate in certain respects to the European Court of Justice.[8]

The Lord Chancellor's concern was to ensure that the UK should see exactly what sovereignty sacrifices were necessary, and how serious the loss would be. Other officials acknowledged the loss of sovereignty, stating that:

> In the past, the loss of national sovereignty has been the most potent argument against British participation in supranational institutions. It was to a large extent responsible for our decision, in 1950, not to join the European Coal and Steel Community and, in 1955, to withdraw from the discussions which led

> eventually to the drafting of the Treaty of Rome. Although the Treaty of Rome does not express this explicitly, it has underlying political objectives, which are to be brought about by a gradual surrender of sovereignty.[9]

In June and July of 1961 Macmillan consulted with the Commonwealth about British entry. In July the Cabinet agreed to open negotiations with the Six. Macmillan announced his decision to Parliament on 31 July, giving an undertaking that he would consult Parliament before entering into any agreement. On 9 August 1961 Macmillan formally submitted Britain's first application to join the EEC and the negotiations opened in October. On 14 January 1963, after intense negotiations, President de Gaulle vetoed Britain's application. His reasons could have been endorsed by Eden:

> England in effect is insular, she is maritime, she is linked through her exchanges, her markets, her supply lines to the most diverse and often the most distant countries; she pursues essentially industrial and commercial activities, and only slight agricultural ones. She has in all her doings very marked and very original habits and traditions.
>
> The question is whether Great Britain can now place herself like the Continent and with it inside a tariff which is genuinely common, to renounce all Commonwealth preferences, to cease any pretence that her agriculture be privileged, and, more than that, to treat her engagements with other countries of the free trade area as null and void – that question is the whole question.[10]

Wilson and Heath, 1964–1973

Following Labour's 1964 General Election victory, Michael Palliser, Private Secretary for Foreign Affairs to the prime minister, announced that Labour was conducting a 'genuine reappraisal' of its European policy and concluded that 'though the consequences of early entry' may seem 'economically bleak, the long-term economic consequences of continuing on our present relatively independent course look much bleaker; and as time passes, the difficulty and price of entering the Community will both grow greater'.[11]

By the spring of 1967 Wilson was determined to join and, together with Foreign Secretary George Brown, went on an official tour of the European capitals to guage opinion. Britain's second application to join the EEC was formally submitted on 10 May 1967, only to be vetoed again by de Gaulle in November.

Following the resignation of de Gaulle in 1969 and the election of Edward Heath in 1970, a flash of sunlight pierced through the clouds and the membership mojo went into top gear. The primary objective of the Conservatives, following their 1970 General Election victory, was to secure entry. Heath expressed his 'belief in the general benefit for Europe, as well as for Britain, of our being a full, and full-hearted, member'.[12] To achieve this, Heath established the European Secretariat in the Cabinet Office and the third leg of Britain's negotiations began. Heath inherited Labour's negotiating team and proceeded on that basis between July 1970 and January 1972.

The Conservatives' White Paper,[13] stressing the economic and political benefits of entry, was published on 7 July 1971. It conceded that food prices would rise and that Britain's contribution to the EEC budget may become a burden, unless the Common Agricultural Policy (CAP) was reformed. The White Paper also reinforced the Churchill view of national sovereignty. 'What is proposed', it claimed, 'is a sharing and an enlargement of individual national sovereignties in the general interest.' Con O'Neill declared that Britain's priority was 'to get into the Community, and thereby restore our position at the centre of European affairs which, since 1958, we had lost'.[14]

Meanwhile, in May 1971 following a meeting between Heath and Pompidou, the French President signalled that the veto would be lifted and that a third application would be successful. Just as Churchill, Eden and Macmillan had trimmed their views to appease the Conservative Party, Wilson had to manage his recalcitrant left-wingers who saw the EEC as little more than a capitalist club. However, led by Roy Jenkins, 69 Labour MPs voted in favour. Led by Enoch Powell, 39 Conservative MPs voted against. In May 1971, the vote was passed. In 1972 the Treaty of Rome was signed and on 1 January 1973 Britain entered the EEC and returned to its place on the European stage.

The hope that Britain's entry would settle the issue of Britain and Europe was not realised. Wilson went into both general elections in 1974 with a pledge to renegotiate the terms of membership and to put the decision to the British people. In March 1975 following the conclusion of the renegotiations, the Cabinet voted 16–7 in favour of continued membership. When the decision was presented to the House of Commons, it received a large majority, mainly due to Conservative support. On the Labour side, 137 voted for continued membership, while 145 MPs voted against and 33 abstained. The decision was put to the proof in 1975 when the country voted two to one in favour of staying in. Britain's 20-year retreat from Empire seemed to have been signed, sealed and delivered in favour of a new European future.

But with an EEC which had achieved very little in itself in its 20 years of life, it was not surprising that Britain ended up with a rickety European/post-imperial fudge. This constructive ambiguity as to why the UK had joined ensured that the next 20 years posed the question as to whether Britain would ever really stay in the club.

Early attempts by the UK to persuade Europe to recapture Churchill's vision and Eden's pragmatism in the conduct of its business were thwarted by the mid-1970s oil crisis and domestic turmoil. Jim Callaghan expressly refused to join the European Monetary System in 1978. Ironically, given what was to happen next, this policy was denounced by Margaret Thatcher as hopelessly un-*communautaire* and driven by Labour's left wing.

The leader about to enter the story did not see the economic case as the sole reason for membership. She said 'the paramount case for being "in" is the political case for peace and security … The Community opens windows on the world for us that since the war have been closing.'[15]

Before her election, the Conservatives were Europe's party. They were to be for a long while yet as Thatcher sought to revive again Churchill's three circles.

Churchill revisited: A new vision for Britain's relationship with Europe, the US and the Commonwealth

Identifying the core principle of Thatcherism in 1982, Brian Walden, host of the signature Sunday political programme *Weekend World*, stated it was none other than a 'Britain resurgent'. This was a spine-tingling challenge to declinism and despair, a message which brought old imperialists and young patriots together.

When Thatcher took power in 1979, Britain was the sick man of Europe. By 1990, it was forging a new model of prosperity and a new global vision. During that decade Thatcher would seek new meaning to the imaginative policy lost at Suez. She would attempt to revive Churchill's three circles with a belief in the redemptive power of the British state, the transformative power of liberal economics and the global power of the Anglosphere. By 1990, lauded in the newly liberated capitals of Eastern Europe, Thatcher had become an icon of a new age, not the beggar at others' feasts.

During the 1980s, a renaissance was achieved. Thatcher sought to revive the special relationship by participating in a united effort with the US to defeat the Soviet Union and promote democracy. She sought the same in Europe by forging a single market and a single foreign policy. Renewed efforts to engage the Commonwealth were undertaken following the independence of Zimbabwe in 1980, but, in the end, the battle over apartheid meant the institution declined in importance.

Thatcher brought a change of style to Britain's relationship with Europe but it was a rhetorical rather than substantive change.

During her three terms in office Thatcher 'took Britain further into Europe than anyone except Heath.'[16] She did so with Churchillian rhetoric and vision with which she sought to empower herself and enthuse fellow leaders.

Her aim in government was not to leave Europe, but to lead it. She wanted to shape a different Europe. She was way ahead of her time in her belief that Europe's nations had to remain the bedrock of its legitimacy and that Britain's role was to open the continent to the world. Her vision of an enlarged Europe – with emphasis on open markets and economic reform – is now expounded by most member states. No European governments today still advocate pan-European federalism.

Thatcher also wanted to create a European defence and foreign policy, saying: 'I am the first to say that on many great issues the countries of Europe should try to speak with a single voice.'[17] She saw British leadership as the political glue that would keep American-led NATO and the defence of the continent firmly together. Commission president, Roy Jenkins, mused that Thatcher saw the EEC and NATO as two bodies 'that should be amalgamated.'[18]

And Europe was ready to listen. The German Chancellor, Helmut Schmidt, was a convinced Anglophile. He wanted an imaginative British European strategy based on smart power. His successor, Helmut Kohl, sought to re-ignite Churchill's European vision. On a visit to Chequers in 1984, he agreed with Thatcher on the need to link Britain's military hard power with geopolitical soft power, to be achieved by Germany, France and the UK acting together to project smart power in the world. Kohl argued that the Treaty of Rome should not be conceptually limited to the benefits of a common market. As the world changed, Europe needed to act together on defence and foreign policy. He foresaw that the United States would look west to deal with China, rather than east to deal with Russia. He urged Britain to examine the value of Europe, not just its price.

As we shall see, the achievements of Thatcher and her successor, John Major, in creating a new Europe are historical fact, but lost in the Eurosceptic myth of defiance and defeat. The deep irony is that today Lady Thatcher is lionised as the founder of modern Euroscepticism, the Boudicca of the bourgeoisie. Becoming a refusenik from her own and her successors' governments reinforced her image as the heroine who would battle for Britain till her dying breath. Anti-Europeanist nationalism is alleged to be the blood that coursed through her body politic. But little can be further from the truth.

In 1961, Thatcher advocated a position which would become held by the pro-Europeans: 'Sovereignty and independence are not ends in themselves,' she told the Finchley Conservatives. 'It is no good being independent in isolation if it involves running down our economy and watching other nations outstrip us both in trade and influence.'[19]

What is surprising is both how visionary and how subtle the Thatcher government was in grasping this approach. British leadership in Europe was yet again on offer. But from 1985 Germany was driven unwillingly into the French orbit through British indifference, and from 1990 the French tightened their grip on Germany through the single currency. Why then did Britain's success in reshaping Europe in the years after 1985 lead to diplomatic isolation and political disaster?

Smart power

During Margaret Thatcher's ten years in power, Britain fought three critical battles which, while aimed at reviving Europe, were to make, then break, her political leadership, turning the Conservative attitude to Europe on its head.

(1) **Smart spending v. wasteful spending:** The first objective of Thatcher's European policy was to instil rigour into a European budgetary practices criticised for excess. Britain sought to ensure that the EEC's reputation was no longer hindered by the waste represented by butter mountains and wine lakes. Revising Britain's contribution to the EU Budget was the beginning of this process. After several

years of negotiations the 1984 Fontainebleau Agreement established a correction mechanism for dealing with budgetary imbalances, while Britain was granted her rebate. Britain's success changed the member states' approach to the EEC budget.

(2) **Single market v. single currency:** Thatcher's second objective was the creation of a single market, which, through a policy of deregulation, would lead to the formation of a 'free trade and free enterprise area'. By doing so, her aim was to derail the federalist and social democratic plans of Jacques Delors, president of the European Commission from 1985 to 1995, for a social Europe and a single currency. She opposed the European Commission taking advantage of its exclusive powers to initiate legislation. She feared Delors' 1988 prediction that 'in ten years, 80 per cent of economic legislation, and perhaps tax and social regulation, will be directed from the Community'.[20] She denounced Delors' speech delivered to the 1988 TUC at which he called for a social dimension to the Single Market. Britain's success changed the EEC's approach to its economic and social policy. Lord Cockfield, appointed to the European Commission by Thatcher, drove the Single European Act which began the process of launching the Single Market in 1992. But Britain's warnings of the single currency's structural dangers, though unheeded at the time, proved prescient.

(3) **Superpower v. superstate:** Thatcher's third objective was to enhance Europe's regional soft power by leveraging Britain's military and diplomatic clout. Britain and its allies would forge a new approach to Europe's foreign policy. Thatcher sought a wider and more global continent as opposed to a deeper and more bureaucratic project. Thatcher's 1988 Bruges speech proclaimed that 'we have not successfully rolled back the frontiers of the state in Britain, only to see them re-imposed at a European level, with a

> European superstate exercising a new dominance from Brussels.'[21] In the years that followed, Britain's big idea – that the nation states of Europe must spend less time building a superstate and more on delivering hard power in a dangerous region – won increasing support. Britain's warnings about the dangers of excessive top-down *dirigisme* are now accepted.

As we shall see, in all three areas, British leadership has been vindicated and ultimately, if sometimes begrudgingly, accepted. Far from being attempts to thwart Europe, they were aimed at improving continental unity and power. So why are they perceived as failures?

Smart spending v. wasteful spending: 1979–1984

The UK was a major contributor to the budget because of the way the common external tariff and VAT, the EEC's two main sources of financing, were calculated. Because the UK was a large food importer, Britain was faced with paying greater levies on imports than any other member state. So, despite paying in more than anyone else, the British, because of their small and efficient agricultural sector, would also fail to recover from the Community budget. This inequitable situation was compounded by the fact that in the early 1980s nearly 80 per cent of the EEC budget was spent on the CAP, a reputation-busting core policy. Worse still, it caused bizarre inefficiencies regularly pilloried as butter mountains and wine lakes.

This was the *casus belli* Margaret Thatcher used to put Britain on a better footing on a permanent basis. To do so she threatened to use the so-called Luxembourg Compromise to veto Europe's finances. This was a French device used by de Gaulle in 1966 in which if a member state claimed that any decision affected its vital national interests, there would be no vote in the Council of Ministers until a solution was reached. Although not part of the Treaty, member states had effectively accepted it as a de facto way the line against political integration could be drawn.

During May 1982, at the height of the Falklands War, the French decided to ignore Britain's veto card. This drove a coach and horses through Britain's interpretation of the Luxembourg Compromise. Britain would now have to decide whether to turn the cash tap off. Since the EEC could not raise debt it would run out of money. Even Geoffrey Rippon, Heath's right-hand man in the entry negotiations of the early 1970s, weighed in, saying: 'The Community will become a fallen oak if it fails to understand that respect for the Luxembourg Compromise is necessary [to make] the Community work and is essential to its survival.' *The Times* urged caution and compromise. Britain was opening another front: the Falklands War against Argentina and the Budget War against Brussels. 'We are not bad Europeans unless we choose to present ourselves that way,' Rippon[22] said.

Thatcher finessed a strategy which aimed to subtly undermine the CAP by outflanking its protectors with pro-European policies. She appeased the French and Germans by increasing the regional policy budget to finance declining UK industrial areas. She proposed enlarging the EEC to open the European door for British business. In 1983 she offered an increase in the EEC's budget in return for an agreement on the CAP.[23] She also agreed to jointly re-launch the EEC and submitted the seminal paper suggesting that the key policy should be the Single Market. Its aim was to promote the liberalisation of transport, a common market in services, more common European standards and a harmonisation in professional qualifications.

In the subsequent *realpolitik* dance the French president, François Mitterrand, offered a 65 per cent contribution rebate and Margaret Thatcher succeeded in achieving 66 per cent. Although the handbagging myth is propagated proudly by Eurosceptics and remembered ruefully by European administrations, the end result was actually a wafer-thin compromise greeted warmly by the French. The left-wing *Liberation* hailed the British Prime Minister for showing France 'how appallingly badly the Community works'.

This success enabled Thatcher, at the end of the 1984 Fontainebleau summit, to present her vision for the future of Europe. She fired the starting gun on two dynamic and successful policies which were to transform Europe. 'We now must press ahead with both enlargement and the single market which I want to see.' Her aim was to develop the 'full potential of the Community'.[24]

But, in the final analysis, the smart spending v. wasteful spending battle was a pyrrhic victory. Politicians were not ignorant in judging that Brussels-bashing was good copy in the short term, regardless of whether it was bad politics in the long term. What Britain gained in cash, she lost in credibility. Despite Thatcher's positive pronouncements for the future of Europe, she had lost friends and alienated the people who mattered. Though respect for her style was widespread, what irked was that there was no reciprocal respect for why her colleagues wanted European unity in the first place.

Single market v. single currency: 1984–1993

Margaret Thatcher had pulled back from the brink at Fontainebleau. Her advisers were conscious that being labelled a 'bad European' created little but bad blood. Britain had to be more than a grasping *rentier* sitting cross-armed and stony-faced in the corner. As the Conservatives rolled forward the frontiers of free-market capitalism in Britain with the start of the three-pronged privatisation, anti-union and anti-regulation campaign, Thatcher decided her medicine was exactly what Europe needed.

The vision was aimed at creating a 'genuine common market in goods and services' which had been envisaged in the Treaty of Rome, but hardly started in practice. 'Only by a sustained effort to remove remaining obstacles to intra-Community trade can we enable the citizens of Europe to benefit ...'[25]

In 1985 the European Commission published a comprehensive blueprint and timetable for welding together the fragmented national markets to create a genuinely frontier-free single market by the end of 1992. The Schengen Agreement was signed, starting the process of dismantling EU internal border control. The Single European Act was passed by the House of Commons in April 1986. In 1987 the Act came into force clearing the way for decisions and legislation allowing for common laws governing the Single Market. From 1986 to 1992 the EU adopted nearly 280 pieces of legislation to allow 12 sets of national regulations to be replaced by one common European law which would be agreed to in all the member states.

But was the price worth paying? The paradox in this debate is that while Margaret Thatcher was the driving force behind the Single European Act that created the Single Market, it was also the greatest cession of sovereignty in the history of Britain's membership, because of the bonfire of vetoes that it involved. However, Britain accepted the logic of qualified majority voting in order to create the Single Market while ensuring that real power remained in the Council of Ministers where the member states battled to retain control of the European agenda.

But the establishment of the Single Market had led the Community to revive the objective of a social Europe and monetary union. Mitterrand felt that Europe would split if it did not offer something more than pure economics to the people. By now, European unemployment was nearing 20 million. Not least in the UK, the socialist movement had lost faith in the so-called capitalist European project. Mitterrand's France had tried nationalistic Keynesianism which had failed. The British Labour Party went into the 1983 election intent on withdrawing from Europe. Labour voted solidly against the Single European Act when it passed through the Houses of Parliament in 1987. It was a deeply sceptical player in the 1987 General Election. So, it was from a position of fear and weakness that Delors embarked on a political campaign to engage the Germans and the European centre-left in supporting a 'social Europe backed by a single currency'.[26]

Now the trouble began. The non-binding preamble of the Single European Act urged 'concrete steps to the progressive realisation of monetary union'. Article 20 suggested member states cooperate 'in order to ensure the convergence of economic and monetary policies' necessary for the further development of the Single Market. What appeared to be the woolliest of legal texts opened a Pandora's box, in the form of a type of Europe neither Thatcher nor her government desired.

A row developed between Margaret Thatcher and those like Geoffrey Howe who accepted in theory the Delors logic that the Single Market was an economic project which would probably need associated measures such as a rigorous competition policy, transport and energy liberalisation, environmental and social coordination. This 'middle way' Conservative argument was that if there was to be a true single market, it would have to acquire some central regulatory oversight to ensure a competitive environment free of local barriers to trade. After all, it was local barriers to trade that had strangled the attempt to achieve free movement of goods, services, capital and labour which was enshrined in the Treaty of Rome. The European Court of Justice was left with the difficult task of enforcing the free market as the sole institution prepared to ensure the compliance of member states bent on hiding their populations from regional, let alone global, trade.

The Thatcher paradox was that Britain was keen on the 'common market' ends but felt there had been no democratic consent to achieve it through supranational means. The Tory idea was that the Single Market should evolve over time without any immediate and unnecessary surrender of sovereignty. Any attempt to bounce member states into integrationist concepts such as single currency and a single social policy would hijack the economic gains with political aims. At the time this was not only politically difficult to accept, it flew in the face of the economic revolution that Reagan and Thatcher had started. With Britain acting as the twin motor of a new free market economic model that seemed to be delivering results on both sides of the Atlantic, this was out of the question.

In June 1988 European leaders pointed out that 'in adopting the Single Act, the Member States of the Community confirmed the objective of progressive realisation of economic and monetary union.'[27] Delors envisaged the achievement of economic and monetary union in three stages, which ended with national currencies having their convergence rates irrevocably fixed and replaced by the European single currency in 1999.

Still blithe about the seriousness of this agenda, Thatcher let this thin end of the wedge through. As she explained to the House of Commons, progress to monetary union would not necessarily involve a single currency or a European Central Bank because the continentals were beguiled by lofty language and were, in any case, not by any means ready.

Conscious that no formal device to create a single currency existed, Thatcher agreed to these words not because she was duped by Foreign Office federalists but because she was assured by Kohl that he was opposed to giving up the Deustche Mark, the terminology was meaningless and that if any proposal emerged to set Europe on the road to a single currency it would definitely require a treaty change.

Thatcher decided that the best policy in future was to speak softly first and carry a big stick for later: in other words, to allow the European dynamic to continue and wait until greater detail forced more grandiose concepts to wither through their own internal contradictions. Britain would learn the lessons of Fontainebleau and box clever rather than brutal.

So by December 1985, six years into her premiership, Thatcher had returned to Britain with her money back and the Single Market programme on the starting blocks. She had fought two serious campaigns on European soil. On money and the markets she had scored two goals. Although the success of the Single European Act caused little flurry in Britain, it was a copybook British broom-sweeping cure for a Europe that had previously been dominated by special interests and plagued by the gap between its Treaty of Rome 'four freedoms' rhetoric and the protectionist reality. It was to be the first of two historic contributions to Europe by Britain, the second being the enlargement which brought the continent together.

Superpower v. superstate: 1987–1993

With the Soviet Union in retreat, Britain did not stop at a clarion call for the Single Market alone. Margaret Thatcher and her foreign secretary, Geoffrey Howe, moved on from the Single Market to announce a new vision for Europe.

Howe's Foreign Office stated that:

> Membership of the Community could have limited value unless we form part of the inner grouping. The French and the Germans find their relationship by no means easy. Both, for their own reasons, want our participation. Despite … French egocentricity and … confusion in German policy, a determined effort must be made … to attempt to formulate a shared strategy …[28]

Both Thatcher and Howe knew that there existed a Franco-German alliance which wished to act with British support but without the British brake. However, they also knew that the alliance realised that Britain was central to Europe's defence and security and could not be ignored.

So, in a major policy advance, they urged Europe to forget about more treaties to create utopian schemes and move quickly to both complete the Single Market for prosperity and, in a bold move, create a single foreign policy for power. Geoffrey Howe remarked that the way forward for Europe 'does not lie across a paper of institutional schemes. It is through the resourceful use of existing institutions, through pragmatic, flexible, political cooperation that we shall go forward together.'[29] 'We want to see greater unity of Community action in world affairs,' said Margaret Thatcher. 'That is what I understand by a united Europe.'[30]

She joined with Schmidt, Mitterrand and Kohl to clearly support:

- the progressive achievement of a common foreign policy;
- the progressive assumption of greater European responsibility for defence.

She also wanted to keep the 'best aspects' of the CAP, to fund research and development and to allow some to move faster in policy areas than others. She was also ahead of her time in being the first European leader to propose linking environmental policy to economic growth.

By devising a European foreign policy based on enlarging Europe, Britain had crafted a positive, democratic vision to counteract her somewhat negative image as the penny-pinching, small-minded housewife of Europe. This was the creation of a smart-power European foreign policy based on enlarging Europe to welcome new member states.

Her proposals were welcomed by the French and Germans as a significant step forward in British policy on Europe. To Paris and Berlin this presaged a new era in British involvement.

In Berlin, Britain's vision cemented a relationship. It matched Kohl's Anglophile vision of strengthening the transatlantic alliance through better Western European coordination. Better still, Thatcher and Kohl saw Europe as a model for freedom whose grand strategy was to act as a democratic magnet for enlargement as it had just done for Spain and Portugal, who joined in 1986.

In Paris, Britain's vision was welcomed for its grandeur. The French Government liked the idea that the institutional big bang that brought down barriers to trade could also be a vehicle to empower their thwarted European leadership not only in defence and foreign policy but on social Europe and the single currency.

As the British Embassy in Paris reported: 'What then is involved in … European Union? The delight for [the French] is that one does not really have to know or say. There are several advantages they can see in a large bag of wind labelled European Union: leadership.'[31]

So, in 1985, with these two policies in play, Thatcher and Howe, with the tacit support of Kohl, proposed a joint European foreign policy backed by a new institution. The Germans agreed to triangulate Paris's ideas for 'social Europe' and London's for foreign policy coordination. They called it the 'European Union'.

There was one problem. Unlike Thatcher, Kohl and Mitterrand feared that, with enlargement, the seeds of Europe's eventual destruction were being sowed. An ever larger union would be less coherent and more prone to split. What France and Germany feared was not at all a loss of federal momentum towards a unified future but a potentially violent retreat to the 1930s. The French and Germans were stumbling towards the idea that if Europe went a little deeper, it would help it to withstand going a little wider.

The question unresolved at this point was what did deeper mean? The British offered the Single Market and foreign policy; the French offered a single currency and social Europe. The Germans offered the structure that they thought would make both work better. To resolve the issue, in 1985 an intergovernmental conference (IGC) was called to discuss Europe's future at the highest political level.

At this stage, Britain could have moved forward to construct an Anglo-German *entente* on the basis of the substantial common ground between the countries. Britain could have agreed to the summit and either played Germany off against France or vice versa. But, whereas most member states thought the Treaty of Rome would need amending to accommodate these different strains of thought, Britain, fearful of French ideas finding their way into the legislative process, did not want a treaty change to be on the agenda and decided to vote against the summit. Not enough allies – beyond the Danes and the Greeks – were assembled. They lost. Britain, despite leading the debate, had forsaken the tactical battle and been outflanked. The fight for Europe's future – as a superpower or a superstate – had begun.

After this strategic setback there were three leaps into full-blown Euroscepticism. The first was Bruges, the second was the consequences of the fall of the Berlin Wall in 1989 and the third was the battle over the Maastricht Treaty in 1993. The Conservatives, punch-drunk from 50 years of bewildering decline but revived by the hallucinatory drugs of post-imperial renaissance, were now awakening to their cause, but forsaking the opportunities that Margaret Thatcher had created.

The Bruges vision

The trouble in Britain began in Bournemouth. In order to make Europe palatable to the hostile Labour Party and trade unions, in

September 1988 Delors appeared at the TUC conference promising a new field of battle where they could raise their tattered socialist flag. Social and employment policy was on its way to Brussels and Delors unfurled an irresistible vision for the left. Adding salt to the wounds, Delors foolishly mused that, in time, 80 per cent of national legislation would derive from Europe and that the EU had a manifest destiny.

So facing another European battle, Margaret Thatcher decided it was time for a repeat of her earlier vision. Less than a month after the Delors speech came Thatcher's counterattack. She stepped up at the College of Europe to deliver her *coup de grâce* to the pretensions of the Commission President. Her speech tried to synthesise the positive policy proposals of the previous four years to portray the vision many thought was lacking but, because it was made as the waves of integration swelled, it became one of the defining moments of British Euroscepticism.

Thatcher's warning about a 'European superstate exercising a new dominance from Brussels' and that 'Britain will fight collectivism and corporatism at the European level,'[32] excited her supporters and sent shudders around the continent. But, the speech spelled out the Thatcherite position clearly:

- National sovereignty is paramount over supranational bodies.
- Europe is led by its member states which cooperate transnationally when required.
- Supranational norms cannot override national parliaments or judiciaries.
- The European Commission should lose its power of legislative initiative to the Council of Ministers.

It was, in fact, a standard repeat of British policy on Europe, not only from Chamberlain and Churchill but straight through to Major and Blair.

Reading it nearly 30 years later, it is striking how the Europe she painted is, in fact, with us now. Many European leaders today would find it impossible to disagree with its main precepts. Not because they simply agree with them, but that much of what she said has actually come to pass.

Reviving her grand foreign policy idea, Thatcher paved the way for Britain's second historic policy change in Europe – enlargement. By mentioning Warsaw, Prague and Budapest as great European cities, she urged a wider, not a deeper, Europe with NATO as the continent's defence cornerstone.

If the other member states agreed with this prospectus, then Britain could seize anew the mantle of European leadership. If they did not, the battle over the future of Europe would continue. Thatcher had done the historic equivalent of Martin Luther nailing his 95 Theses of Contention to the Wittenberg church door. A year later the Berlin Wall fell and her vision was no longer a pipe dream. Europe was there for the making again.

The continental vision

Few people can forget today how revolutionary the events were that took place between 1989 and 1991 in the history of Europe, let alone of the world. The collapse of the Berlin Wall brought the whole of Central and Eastern Europe into political play for the first time since 1945. At one stroke the European civil war that had begun 75 years before with a pistol shot in Sarajevo was over.

The lights were coming on again one by one all over Europe. Within two years the Soviet Union was gone, swept away from the iron curtain to distant borders. At the heart of this maelstrom stood Germany, reunited in October 1990. The country that had done so much to make, then destroy, Europe's power and reputation was rich, huge and unshackled. Nobody at the beginning of 1989 would have predicted that, by year's end, Europe's destiny would be up for grabs.

Few however also remember that these events heralded a revolutionary change in the battle between Thatcher's vision of Europe as a superpower to project and protect the Bruges values of democracy, freedom and the rule of law, and Mitterrand's need for a superstate to control Germany. Dealing with the new Germany and its consequences instigated a half-time change in the rules of the game, which, far from enhancing Britain's chance to dominate Europe, destroyed it. It was German unification that was the most deadly source for Euroscepticism. It was fear of a German Europe driven by an historical Prussian need for mechanistic unity that revived old myths for new times.[33]

The scene shift began with the quiet agreement between Mitterrand and Thatcher that it was far better for both of them that Germany should be on its knees. If not, she would soon be at their throats. One month after the fall of the wall, the two leaders met at the Strasbourg European Council. Thatcher's utopian views were gently brushed aside by the French President. Germany was now free to roam and had the money and commercial power to do so. They had to do something about the Germans. First, they had to stop reunification.

As after Suez, how to deal with Germany would set London and Paris from the same place on two different roads to achieve the same goal. The same place was a genuine fear of German power. Jacques Attali, Mitterrand's key adviser, told John Major that he expected Germany to get nuclear weapons by the turn of the new century, dominate Eastern Europe and emerge as a co-world leader with the US, the USSR and Japan. Such opinions added to Margaret Thatcher's own fears.

The problem was not the diagnosis, however erroneous it subsequently proved, but the cure. For the French, Germany's political power must be anchored within the European structure and that meant diluting Berlin's room for manoeuvre within 'political union'. Germany's economic power must be equally anchored in Europe and that meant diluting the Deutsche Mark in a single currency. Jacques Delors, tactfully avoiding the real reasons behind this, dressed policy up in eurospeak:

> Strengthening the Community means pressing ahead with implementing the Single Act. But now this alone is not enough. The pace of change is gathering momentum and we must try to

> keep up. Only a strong, self-confident Community … can truly help to control that process. So we need progress on two fronts: monetary union and political cooperation …[34]

What he meant was: the superpower idea was fine for yesterday, but now the Germans are on the march and we've got to bind them down economically and politically and a superstate is the way to do it because that's what the Germans want too.

This was the trade-off. The Germans would sell their currency to buy reunification and the French would sell their sovereignty to buy the Germans. So in December 1989 the heads of government said that at the next IGC in April 1990 the programme for economic and monetary union would be agreed and a date set for the next IGC to agree political union.

Suddenly, though both Britain and France agreed on the problem, Margaret Thatcher flatly refuted the French solution. Binding Germany into Europe meant handing Europe to Germany. As far as she was concerned, it was no different a concept than binding Warsaw, Prague and Budapest to Moscow, an integration process now unravelling before the eyes of the world. Why propose centralisation when history was motoring in the opposite direction? But the British failed to offer any alternative bar a back-to-the-future balance of power game where the *entente cordiale* would stop reunification at best and keep a political watch on the Rhine at worst.

At the Dublin IGC she amplified this holding strategy by trying to persuade member states that economic union could be achieved by having a common currency which could evolve into a single currency and that political union could be achieved by ensuring that the Council of Ministers would continue to make decisions and the European Parliament would continue to make noise. Add into this a clear definition of subsidiarity which would keep nation states sovereign and the British would be happy.

But by April 1990 the idea was one year too late. Thatcher failed to factor in that the urgency was no longer economic but political.

The British European commissioner, Leon Brittan, reflected that, if indeed this was a political process, the only way to achieve her objective to control Germany was to ally with the French from inside the structures of economic union, not outside. In other words, to join the process. She was therefore caught between the devil and the deep blue sea.

Having lost the battle over the single currency, Thatcher accused the EEC of attempting to 'extinguish democracy', while introducing a federal Europe 'by the back door'. To many, Thatcher had crossed the Rubicon. Moreover, Thatcher's increasingly sceptical position on the EEC was at odds with public opinion, which, following a period of opposition in the early 1980s, was generally supportive of continued membership by 1990. German demons did not trouble the British. By November that year she was tripped up by history and toppled by her own Cabinet.

Following Thatcher's succession by John Major, the Conservative anti-European faction grew in numbers and strength, exploiting the government's narrow majority of 21 after the 1992 General Election. Major's policy was to carry on with Thatcher's intergovernmental and market economy-based Europe but with rhetorical balm to put Britain 'at the heart of Europe'.

But Major was faced with four irreconcilable problems:

(1) His victory required him to appease the pro-Europeans who had reacted so vocally to Thatcher's own growing Euroscepticism.
(2) He was tied personally to the one integrationist policy which Thatcher had been forced to accept – sterling's membership of the European Exchange Rate Mechanism (ERM).
(3) Some of his MPs could now coalesce around Bruges as Thatcher's Eurosceptic Sermon on the Mount, in order to protect her flame. Any backsliding by Thatcher's chosen successor on Europe would be toxic.

(4) Jacques Delors now proposed the high-water-mark big bang integrationist project in the form of the Maastricht Treaty which would turbo-charge the social, monetary and economic supranationalism which Thatcher feared.

At first he succeeded in spinning the plates. His Maastricht negotiations secured opt-outs from two of the three supranationalisms. In a significant achievement, Major achieved what the Conservatives wanted if the Europeans failed to swallow the Bruges doctrine: a two-speed Europe.

Then, on 16 September 1992, the pound was humiliatingly ejected from the ERM by inflexible Germans and unhelpful French. For the Conservatives, it was game, set and match to Thatcher's view on Europe. Major was now the hapless cuckoo in the Tory nest. History had dealt him the worst hand. He was not only considered naive and wrong; he was a patsy, not a leader.

By 1996, 74 Conservative MPs voted in favour of Bill Cash's 'thus far and no further without a referendum'. Major's Europe was over before it had started. In the 1997 General Election, he was defeated by a landslide.

The Blair vision

After the paralysis of the Major government's European policy, the New Labour government dusted off the forgotten Thatcher superpower file and tried again to re-orient Britain as a leading member state of Europe, with a positive agenda of European enlargement, military integration/modernisation and a new doctrine of 'liberal interventionism'. London would metamorphose into an Atlanticist power pole around which Europe would cluster. New Labour promised to put Britain at the heart of Europe and seek, with the Commonwealth and the United States, to forge the three circles anew.

The Blair and Brown governments sought to establish British 'leadership' within Europe untroubled by the intra-party divisions that prevented such an approach under the Major government. In a speech at Chatham House in April 1995 Blair reiterated the view that Britain's global influence was dependent on influence in Europe and resolved to focus on two areas: finally taking European leadership in defence and foreign policy and completing the Single Market.

But there was to be one problem. Faced with a Eurosceptic press and the imperative of re-election New Labour tried to depoliticise the European issue. The end result was that while Britain re-engaged in Europe and led in economic and security policies little progress was achieved domestically in establishing public support for this more constructive revival of Churchill's dream. The idea was to be electorally defensive at home, while undertaking a more aggressive diplomacy abroad.[35]

The December 1998 Anglo-French initiative at St Malo on giving Europe a stronger defence identity set the agenda for what became the European Security and Defence Policy. The March 2000 agreement at the Lisbon European Council saw Britain succeeding in gaining a pan-European commitment on a strategy designed to transform Europe into a dynamic knowledge-based economy.

But over the course of the New Labour years, this early promise evaporated. Britain became unable to occupy the central position in Europe's policy agenda that it first sought. The success of British initiatives between 1997 and 2003 was undermined by Blair's support for President George W. Bush's foreign policy after the 9/11 terrorist attacks. This opened up dangerous gaps with the allies that Blair had painstakingly brought behind the British agenda. Unresolved divisions between Atlanticist member states and Gaullists headed by French president Jacques Chirac were laid bare in US Secretary of Defense Donald Rumsfeld's unhelpful comment that the new divide was between 'old Europe' and 'new Europe'. The Blair government found its efforts to act as a bridge between the US and Europe impossible to sustain. It had to take sides and on Iraq chose that of President Bush.

Iraq undermined the goodwill in British relations with France and Germany, and this badly affected the government's efforts to shape Europe's agenda. Also, the war began a long-term decline in Blair's domestic popularity which made him more defensive on areas of European policy, particularly when confronting Britain's Eurosceptic press.

However, it was not only the distraction of foreign wars which set back the Blair approach. He suffered the misfortune of timing which had also bedevilled Churchill, Eden and Thatcher before him. Two issues – the euro and the Constitutional Treaty – were divisive policies which reinvigorated Euroscepticism and saw New Labour caught between its instinctive push for leadership and its fear of the electoral consequences.

This was evident in New Labour promoting the virtues of both the single currency and the constitution, but subjecting both to a referendum. One was not required on the euro after Chancellor Gordon Brown announced on 9 June 2003 that Britain would not be joining. Then in April 2004 Blair decided the government would put the EU's forthcoming Constitutional Treaty to a referendum, seeking both to neutralise the Treaty as an issue and construct a domestic consensus from the fruits of his government's constructive European policy. The French and Dutch rejections of the Constitutional Treaty in May/June 2005 meant that Blair was denied the chance to win the battle over Britain's place in Europe.

Blair's swansong came during the British presidency of the EU in the second half of 2005. Blair made a major speech to the European Parliament in Strasbourg on 23 June 2005. He sought in the aftermath of the two referendum results on the Constitutional Treaty to offer a new vision for Europe, calling for reform to its economic and social policies to make it more relevant to future global challenges. He questioned whether the constitutional debate had brought Europe closer to the people, as had been the intention. The speech was a lucid and powerful reinforcement of Britain's view since the war:

> The broad sweep of history is on the side of the European Union. Countries round the world are coming together today because in collective cooperation they increase individual strength.

> The United States is the world's only superpower. But within a few decades China and India will be the world's largest economies, each of them with populations three times that of the whole of the European Union. The idea of Europe, united and working together, is essential today for our nations to be strong enough to keep our place in this world.
>
> But now we have to renew. If we do not, if Europe defaulted to Euroscepticism, or if European nations, faced with the immense challenge we have in front of us, decided to huddle together, hoping we can avoid globalisation, shrink away from confronting the changes around us, take refuge in the present policies of Europe as if by constantly repeating them, we would by the very act of repetition make them more relevant, then we risk failure. Failure on a grand, strategic scale. The people of Europe are speaking to us.

He famously concluded by urging on Europe a reality check and to receive the wake-up call:

> The people are blowing the trumpets around the city walls. Are we listening? They are posing the questions. They are wanting our leadership and it is time we gave it to them. Have we the political will to go out and meet them so that they regard our leadership collectively as part of the solution, and not part of the problem?[36]

No. The problem was that for all New Labour's dynamic rhetoric in Europe, both Blair and Brown failed to sell any such vision at home. Blair feared the print media and failed to lead in the one area that he wanted to – namely, as a changemaker. In a speech in Aachen in summer 1999 he remarked that, 'I have a bold aim … That over the next few years Britain resolves once and for all its ambivalence towards Europe. I want to end the uncertainty, the lack of confidence, the Europhobia.'[37] In this he failed. By the end of his period in office just 36 per cent of respondents in the UK approved of membership of the EU, while 26 per cent did not. Ten years before, the figures had been 34/28 – representing no real change in opinion at all.

Although British influence made progress on policy – on economic competitiveness, climate change, internal security, combating global poverty – New Labour followed previous false starts in failing to exercise smart power through embedding a grand strategy. By 2010 the three circles were no closer to being forged than when Churchill had set them out in 1948.

Decline and fall: Brexit 2016

Since the end of World War II, Britain unfailingly had a European strategy. There is no question that British governments tried to give life to Churchill's dream. Whereas 1979 Britain's room for manoeuvre appeared limited to Europe, the revival of Anglo-America, based, this time, not on power parity but economic and foreign policy symmetry, became a new opportunity. It was from this that the concept emerged of Britain being a bridge, uniting the two circles of Europe and the USA. The objective was to make London a serious participant in European and global affairs by creating unity of purpose between London, Berlin, Paris and Washington.

Though Thatcher and Blair were instinctive pro-Europeans, Thatcher's commitment to the whole idea of British power in Europe was soured by the consequences of German reunification, as was Blair's by the choice he made between the two circles of Europe and America over Iraq. In the confusion which followed, the public's attitude hardened. Thatcher and Blair had both succeeded and failed. They created a vacuum. Stepping into it, in the years that followed the 1997 general election, came the Eurosceptics.

Once David Cameron became prime minister in 2010, any serious effort at engagement withered, and the UK became more absent from both the international and, above all, European theatres. This was due partly to Cameron's foreign policy myopia and partly to the insularity of the Conservative Party he led, whose internal divisions precluded any serious strategic initiative. Britain was on autopilot. Although in every year after 2010 the European Council on Foreign Relations' rating of the soft power of EU member states placed the UK among the top three 'leaders' (as opposed to 'slackers') in foreign policy, this apparent success flattered to deceive. While the UK was capable of piecemeal interventions, particularly regarding sanctions against Russia, the promotion of the Transatlantic Trade and Investment Partnership, Libya, combating ISIS, and providing humanitarian support in the Middle East, it no longer contributed significantly to the great debates on the future of Europe.

The then French foreign minister Laurent Fabius openly complained about the UK's 'non-diplomacy' in Europe, essentially on account of its lack of a coherent policy. A retired British general publicly criticised Cameron for his government's 'irrelevance in foreign policy'. And a highly experienced former British diplomat in the UK and Europe, Robert Cooper, said that Britain seemed to lack both ambition and direction.

This represented a major abdication of power. The reason was that Cameron failed to resolve the infighting between modernisers, traditionalists and nationalists in his party or to rally them behind a neo-Chamberlainite vision that could encompass both a newer global role as America's chief satellite, and an older European role as an Anglo-Saxon Trojan horse, ripping down barriers to commercial and personal freedom. Cameron, as a moderniser, first sought to silence dissent by admonishing his party to stop 'banging on about Europe'. In 2007, he tried a positive vision for Britain's engagement in Europe, the so-called 3G agenda, in which Britain would lead Europe in tacking global warming, global competition and global poverty. But these ideas proved limp and short-lived when confronted with the ideas and the determination of the Eurosceptics.

Feeding the latter's dream were three totemic themes:

First, *economics*. British success in leading a new economic policy and visibly prospering from it in comparison to other European nations meant that the idea of Britain as a world island outside the EU, a model for the rest of the globe, was plausible for the first time since 1956. So Euroscepticism settled into critical opposition to the EU and uncritical support of the USA.

Second, *Bruges*. The defenestration of Margaret Thatcher spurred on Eurosceptics to rally around her cry against a European superstate. It was not relevant that, for all the excitement they felt about the text and tone of Thatcher's 1988 Bruges speech, the vision of Europe as a British-led superpower was forgotten.

Third, *betrayal*. Thatcher's fall enabled Eurosceptics to frame a stab-in-the-back legend consisting of four deceptions:

(1) Britain was deceived when voting for a common market in 1975.
(2) Britain was deceived into believing that the Single European Act was only to create the Single Market.
(3) Britain was deceived about economic and monetary union.
(4) Britain was deceived about the referendum on the EU Constitution.

It was a clear and unambiguous approach was made all the more virulent when, in 2004, UKIP leader Nigel Farage added immigration to the brew. From this flowed the feeling, central to the referendum debate, that Britain had a choice: it could opt for complete freedom of action outside Europe or it could surrender its independence to Brussels. The Bruges speech had been a blueprint for British leadership in Europe. Instead it was used to unleash a new nationalism.

Cameron's problem was that the three-circles policy, which once cloaked Tory disunity, was difficult to reconcile with the identity politics that Euroscepticism represented. The party thus split into modernisers who believed Britain must face up to the world as it is, traditionalists who mourned a nostalgic world that they thought lost but had never been, and nationalists who sought a new world free from diplomatic entanglements. Cameron, the main moderniser, failed either to lead in his earlier proactive scepticism or sideline his opponents.

By 2016 Cameron's failure of leadership meant Eurosceptics fell mostly into the nationalist camp. It was then that the curtain came down. The EU referendum debate was dominated by negative arguments about the costs of staying in or the price of leaving. Even had there been a vote for remaining in the EU, Cameron's failure to build and sustain a positive case to stay based on a long-term revival of British relations with Europe meant that the underlying Euroscepticism that had held Britain back on the international stage would never go away.

Exactly 60 years after Suez, history again brought all the political strands together in one defining incident. Eden's Suez Crisis of 1956 destroyed Churchill's postwar three-circles vision of Britain leading in Europe, the Commonwealth and NATO. Now Cameron's referendum of 23 June 2016 crushed the efforts of Thatcher and Blair to re-forge the three circles with Britain as a bridge between Europe and the United States and the wider world beyond.

The tragic irony of these events 60 years apart is that it was the imperialist Anthony Eden who ended Britain's power as an Empire with his ill-advised Egypt invasion, and it was the pro-European David Cameron who ended Britain's power in the EU with his ill-advised referendum.

But there is one difference: the Empire could never be recovered; Europe can. Britain has to go back to the future. And back to Churchill who said:

> Without Britain there can be no Europe … our friends on the Continent need have no misgivings. Britain is an integral part of Europe, and we mean to play our part in the revival of her prosperity and greatness.[38]

3

Power

What Next?

... in which Britain re-forges Churchill's three circles to revive Britain as a global leader with the Europeans, the United States and the wider world.

> There is all the difference in the world between good-natured, good-humoured effort to keep well in with your neighbours and that spirit of haughty and sullen isolation which has been dignified by the name of 'non-intervention'. We are part of the Community of Europe and we must do our duty as such.
>
> (Lord Salisbury, 1888)[1]

> The trouble with Britain is that it has failed to learn the fine art of persuading others it is fighting for Europe, when all it is really doing is defending its own corner.
>
> (*The Times*, editorial, 1985)

> The world is a big, bad place and the relative importance of Europe's individual states is declining economically and demographically with every passing year. The choice is no longer between national foreign policies and a European foreign policy, but between national irrelevance and collective influence.
>
> (Niall Ferguson, *Daily Telegraph*, 2007)[2]

> The crisis consists precisely in the fact that the old is dying and the new cannot be born; in this interregnum a great variety of morbid symptoms appear.
>
> (Antonio Gramsci)[3]

The end of the beginning for Britain

The British vote was momentous, but it is only the first in a series of fights for the soul of Europe. The outpouring of anger and anti-establishment rancour may only just have begun. The Remain campaign lost the vote not only because their Project Fear failed, but because, for the public, the post-Maastricht European Union seemed close to failure as well. Seen as over-ambitious in its aims, the troubles that globalisation, the constitution, the euro and migration have brought both humbled it and tested the patience of the wider electorate too much. The British, whatever their varied reasons for voting Leave, are not the first country and will not be the last to question their continent's direction in the hands of the EU.

For the UK, this is year zero, again. Britain may have voted to leave an unreformed EU but it did not vote to leave Europe and destroy the national and international order. It voted, in pain, for a change in policy, not, in pleasure, for revolution. The imperative now is to unite the people and the country, not least to keep the West, Europe and Britain secure, democratic and prosperous at a dangerous time. To do so, Britain needs a new vision for itself and Europe. Britain has two choices: turn its back on Europe and face disintegration, or show true leadership in the way it leaves, to reshape its place in a Europe now demanding a new path.

Leaving aside the continuing option of leading change in the EU from within, there are currently two visions on offer: a 'hard Brexit' isolationism involving immediate EU departure – a dead end restricting the UK's influence to its island home; or a 'soft

Brexit' mercantilism, an elite concern restricting the UK's influence to the narrow business of the Single Market. The first reduces Britain to Switzerland, the second to Norway.

If Britain cannot think wider than these two options its influence on the major foreign policy issues of the day will be diminished. Despite the UK being the fifth largest economy in the world, a permanent member of the UN Security Council, a member of the G20 and the G7 and a leading member of NATO, foreign policy influence is about more than the number of top tables a country can sit at. It is also about its ability to craft the outcomes which emerge from within those institutions. Since 1973 Britain's influence has been augmented by its ability to shape the European agenda in Brussels while sharing the same policy objectives prevailing in Washington. The decision to leave the EU means that the bridge between the two capitals will require rebuilding. After Brexit, Britain's empty seat at the decision-making table will deliver a significant blow to British political, economic and commercial stakeholders unless a new policy is created. As the UK's Chancellor of the Exchequer Philip Hammond put it, the UK's views will carry little weight in Europe from now, as the British will have lost their preferred and natural channels of influencing Brussels.

This book proposes a third way, called Smart Brexit, which rejects this course and considers neither Brexit approach ambitious enough. Britain needs a Chamberlainite vision for Britain in the world and a Churchillian one for Britain in Europe, which provides a dynamic and values-driven policy in matters military, diplomatic and commercial. There must be an end to churlish recalcitrance and aimless drift.

Brexit does not require isolation from continental engagement, nor a foreign policy centred for years to come on negotiating nit-picking trade deals aimed at approximating the UK to the commercial position it enjoyed as a full EU member. Britain must be bolder that this. Britain has for centuries been a great European power, and has made sacrifices to ensure that Europe lives under freedom, democracy and the rule of law. With a hard or – to a lesser extent – soft Brexit, Britain potentially denies its own legacy and threatens the stability of the continent. It could destroy the platform on which it can maintain and increase its global influence in the twenty-first century and undermine the present and future foundations of British prosperity. From Pitt to Chamberlain, Churchill to Thatcher, that prospect has been unacceptable.

Smart Brexit, by contrast, aims to turn the UK's European policy back to the political and away from the purely economic sphere where for too long it festered. The threats facing the continent are far bigger than the Brussels-focused mechanics of establishing monetary rules and commercial standards. The Four Freedoms upon which Churchill fought the war – freedom of speech, freedom of religion, freedom from fear and freedom from want[4] – are in peril in and around Europe. Britain can use this moment to step up instead of stepping aside. It can deploy both its hard and soft power to resume its former role as a moral leader of Europe – a bigger Europe than the one focused on realising the EU's more prosaic four freedoms of goods, services, capital and labour.

This will require long-term imagination and short-term guts, but two opportunities arise for Smart Brexit to work.

First, Britain must work with allies to deploy in full its geopolitical assets. There has long been a strong appetite in the United States and among European partners for Britain to shoulder a greater diplomatic, intelligence and military role. Cameron's indifference to this foreign policy reality was a disappointment to all. Britain must *not* now scuttle away from Europe as it did from Empire after 1956. Our allies understand the Brexit vote as reflecting forces which are not just national or European, but global. Most see that there is now no real reconciliation between the opposing views of national democracy and supranational union. In fact, following the referendum, a fundamental split emerged between the Brussels bureaucracy and most of the member states. The governments of the Netherlands, Germany, Italy, Poland, Hungary, Denmark and Sweden, facing the same social and political threats as those that helped decide the UK's referendum, condemned the heads of the Commission and Parliament, who wanted to eject the UK as soon as possible in order to revive their now endangered superstate. They realised that Brussels' calls for 'more Europe' could lead to no Europe at all. A political counter-revolution against the EU is underway. Far from isolating Britain, Brexit is likely to be seen in hindsight as just the first of many tremors leading up to a larger political earthquake that will be felt all over the continent.

Second, Britain must therefore remain active within the European political space. The EU, with its economic focus, is not the only organisation in Europe in which Britain has influence. Despite the fact that its annual budget is smaller than the UK's yearly spending on education, the EU is seen as so all-embracing that people often overlook the multitude of older and newer, smaller and larger intergovernmental organisations rooted in the history of contemporary Europe – many founded and funded by the UK – which continue to help shape its future.

In fact, there is an entire alphabet soup of European organisations in which the UK plays a part:

- European Union (EU)
- Council of Europe (CoE)
- North Atlantic Treaty Organisation (NATO)
- Organisation for Security and Cooperation in Europe (OSCE)
- British–Irish Council
- Organisation for Joint Armament Cooperation (OCCAR)
- Energy Community
- European Patent Organisation (EPO)
- European Science Foundation
- European Organisation for the Safety of Air Navigation (EUROCONTROL)
- International Commission on Civil Status (ICCS)
- Assembly of European Regions (AER)

- EIROforum (CERN)
- Europol
- Agency for International Trade Information and Cooperation (AITIC)
- EUREKA
- European Cooperation in Science and Technology (COST)

Operating in the shadow of the EU and in their own private bubbles they are weak and, mostly, unknown. Together they could provide direction and strength. Rather like the spaghetti of competing private railway lines in the nineteenth century or the profusion of gas and water suppliers in Joseph Chamberlain's Birmingham, these organisations require at least rudimentary coordination – if not consolidation – in order to provide a one-stop shop for the European polity. The specialised character of these organisations adds value to cooperation in Europe beyond the artificial frontiers of the EU and, thereby, provides not only different diplomatic routes but also massive project funding through organisations such as the European Bank for Reconstruction and Development and the Council of Europe Development Bank. But, despite this, as Churchill said of his pudding, together they have no theme.

In those often politically neglected groups – in particular, NATO, the Council of Europe, the European Free Trade Association and the OSCE – as well as the European Free Trade Association, the UK can play a dynamic role in promoting the key values of democracy, freedom and the rule of law.

So, left unchecked, the twin crises of Brexit and EU disharmony could potentially speed up the centrifugal forces leading to political and economic disintegration. Britain could, instead, promote the very 'United Europe' Churchill desired. Not a supranational unification of up to 40 European nations, but a much greater coordination of the many organisations which purport to represent them. To make that point, in 1956 Churchill declared that 'the Europe we seek to unite is all Europe'. For Churchill, recovering the free Europe of his youth and ending the ideological divisions that plagued the continent were the means by which Britain could maintain its status as a Great Power. So the battle that now resumes is between Churchill's Europe, in which no nations are excluded from promoting those key values, and Schuman's Europe, in which those nations which reject the supranational are excluded. And that can only be won by uniting all Europe's disparate agencies. As Churchill said: 'Upon this battle depends the future of Western civilization.'

For Britain, the untold tale of this identity crisis is that the British people long for someone to have a clear idea for their country's future. British Influence's polling shows the public want Britain to show a lead in Europe and work together with other countries to change it. A great prize in British politics awaits the political party that can build a big-tent agenda with a strong, forward policy for the country. So, there is no point in throwing the European baby out with the Brexit bathwater.

The beginning of the end for the EU?

Another reason not to throw the baby out with the bathwater is that, as many member states acknowledge, the EU is now an idea in crisis. Having failed so far to mitigate the worst effects of globalisation, too many of its citizens across the continent face economic stagnation or worse, and too many feel forgotten and culturally repudiated. The EU promised that constituent nations could flourish and prosper under a shared economic aegis and the euro. Their perceived failure to have done so is causing a populist and nationalist revolt. By conflating a troubled common currency with its core purpose, the EU is struggling to find an institutional solution to a problem the public blames it for creating.

Hence the crisis is also existential. Up till now there have been only two basic models for the EU. The first was to keep to the present loose union of self-governing states with a separation of powers between the supranational and the intergovernmental.

This division, long supported by the UK, was also acceptable to many other member states and mostly retained public consent. But it always grated against the second model of a federal union, conceived by Robert Schuman, in which the EU would be central to European governance. His concept of finally achieving peace on the continent by integrating European economies was considered as the first rung on the ladder of his version of a united Europe. But progress after the 1957 Treaty of Rome focused inexorably on the economic, not the political. The means to a political end became a purely economic end in its own right. Although dressed up in the language of federal unity, member states kept control of the key levers of real power, ceding only what was necessary to achieve continental economies of scale and maintain global competitiveness. The high-water mark was reached with the Single European Act of 1986, which created the Single Market, and the Maastricht Treaty, which set the euro in motion. But, by 2005, when first the French and then the Dutch rejected the political endgame of the Constitutional Treaty, the federalist tide began to ebb. Serious differences emerged about the best way forward. Was there to be more enlargement (which France opposed) or more integration (which Britain and others opposed)? But just as economic integration was reaching the limits of public consent, a crisis exploded to which only more economic integration was the solution.

The 2011 Eurozone debacle brought to a head the stand-off between the intergovernmentalists and the federalists. In order to save the Eurozone, even the British government acknowledged that the practical need for fiscal consolidation would logically require a Eurozone government in which the ECB would replace the need for national central banks, and trade, economic, industrial and social policies would require a federal authority.

But any drive for a unitary European state, imposed as a remedy for the ongoing crisis of the common currency, would, paradoxically, command no common democratic consent, and risk deep political fracture in many European nations. With memories of World War II now faded and the threat of war between Western European countries gone, people are more sceptical and confused about what the EU is for. Worse still, they distrust their political leaders, who seem in limbo, pulling hopelessly at the old rhetorical levers, but unable to define the EU's new purpose in a changing world.

Even before the UK referendum, Europe-wide public hostility to ceding further control over their domestic economies had intensified. Since the euro came into force, of fourteen referenda held on the EU in member states, nine have been lost. Those countries that retain their own currency and remain in control of foreign and defence policies have resisted any further merging of the two models.

With Brexit, the EU's loss of economic self-confidence and political momentum has worsened. The crisis has revealed that the EU does not have a manifest destiny to grow into a regional, federal bloc governed by supranational means. Asymmetric shocks like the financial crisis have blocked the trajectory. The 'ever closer union' EU model has been unable to weather these storms. It remains stuck trying to make sense of the contradictions between deeper economic integration and wider enlargement. Without long-term leadership from London, Paris and Berlin, the EU has failed to apply political will to Europe's duty to maintain stability at home and abroad while being a co-leader in global governance.

Britain, Europe and the world

If this wasn't bad enough, with the EU now in a period of stasis, the rules of the global game are changing dramatically around it. Turbo-charged historical transformation is gathering pace. This is not only a result of the rise of China, the revanchism of Russia or chaos in the Middle East and north Africa, but of the decline of a West in which Britain has played a leading part for 500 years.

The nervous breakdown implicit in Dean Acheson's chilling phrase that Britain has 'lost an empire but not yet found a role' is no longer restricted to Britain. The geopolitical reversal of fortune suffered by Britain is now shared with Europe and, to a lesser extent, the USA. A frightening economic and demographic revolution is underway which will see an upended world by 2050.

Although Britain is estimated to become the largest and richest European nation by 2050, the West will boast only 12 per cent of the global population. Only half of that again will be Europeans. Meanwhile, by 2050, the West's share of global output will have reduced by over half compared to its 1950 share (from 68 per cent to 30 per cent), a level last seen in 1800 when China and India lost their status as the world's economic superpowers. Without question, the West's centrality in world affairs is in decline as cracks appear in its political unity. The trials of Platonic late-stage democracy mixed with Carroll Quigley's seventh 'decay' stage of civilisational evolution is an unenviable backdrop against which to turn the European tanker around.[5]

Faced with such geopolitical challenges, the United States may see the defence of the European arm of the West as superfluous to its own more Pacific-orientated policy, especially if Europe is incapable of rising to the occasion. If it cannot assemble the economic or political will to defend its eastern and southern frontier, the United States is unlikely to protect indefinitely a continent that provides more problems than solutions. Indeed, American indifference may only be exacerbated as it faces its own era of relative decline.

It is therefore imperative that, faced with such world-changing demographic, economic and political upheavals, the United States, Britain and Europe create a much more cohesive response. Isolationism, in which Britain bobs and weaves its way around these threats, will be pointless while the revisionist Eastern powers seek to divide the West in order to rule the twenty-first century. If the West divides itself and fails to unite and confront the challenges of a globalised world it can no longer master, then we reach an endgame predicted by Quigley where 'the civilisation, no longer able to defend itself because it is no longer willing to defend itself lies wide open … to another, younger, more powerful civilisation'.[6]

The prize

Despite this baleful situation, the game is on again. The Brexit vote is not the beginning of the end for British influence. Britain and the West's ideological, cultural, commercial and military assets are vast. A civilisation which boasts the Magna Carta, the Renaissance, the Scientific Revolution, the Enlightenment, parliamentary democracy, modernity and the values of democracy, freedom and the rule of law creates a smart-power magnetic pull on all parts of the world.

The 500-year advance of European culture has entrenched English as the world's lingua franca. Several other European languages, including French, Spanish and Portuguese, are spoken throughout many of the world's nations. Combined with the cultural vigour of European democracies – especially in cinema, sport, music, drama and the arts – a profound impression of soft power is conveyed across the globe. Nominally protecting this legacy stand the hard military and diplomatic power of the United States, the United Kingdom and France – still seen as champions of freedom and civilisation leaders.

In fact, while the United States is the top military power, the United Kingdom and France have the fifth- and seventh-biggest defence budgets in the world. Combined, all European countries spend a total of approximately £190 billion each year – more than Asia and 14 times more than Africa. Although the 1.5 million European soldiers in uniform would, if united and well-armed, represent a formidable force, only the UK and France are resourced for power projection.

Europe also still packs a formidable economic punch. Its 500 million people created over £14 trillion of GDP in 2014, making it the world's largest single market. European cities have seized the opportunities of the globalised economy, none more so than London. London boasts more international corporate headquarters and foreign banks than any other comparable city. Together, London and Paris produce over £600 billion each year, an amount bigger than the GDP of Russia or Sweden.[7]

So 2016 heralds the possibility of serious change to transform Britain's role in Europe and thereby the world. Britain has the ultimate sovereignty to disengage from the EU, but British governments have always concluded that it is in the national interest to play a role on the continent. But the debate changes as the world changes. In the 1950s the Empire remained the sole elixir of power as far as the British establishment was concerned. The American alliance also underpinned Britain's power and global role. Fifty years later, the Empire and the Soviet Union are gone, and the Thatcher–Reagan revolution, a 30-year *tour de force* which changed the world, is over. And, with the era of liberal interventionism now broken in the deserts of Iraq and Afghanistan, it is vital to discover a new sense of urgency and a new rhetoric for the British state in Europe.

Britain's active re-engagement with the continent could enable her to leverage Europe as a top global power. To do so, Britain and her European allies need to accept that the limits of Schuman's dream have been reached and that, in the areas of foreign, security and defence policy, there is little will to unify policy at a supranational level. Timidity in some EU states, and the need for unanimity in the projection of force, mean that European power will continue to be a NATO and thereby nation-state-led policy, resolved, more often than not, outside the EU structure.

Britain has always known that Europe's collective military power is greater than the EU's influence. This is, after all, why Tony Blair and Jacques Chirac – after the EU's failure to deal with the breakdown of Yugoslavia – started the alignment of their armed forces at St Malo in 1998, a process which resulted in the Anglo-French Treaty of 2010. The aim was to demonstrate to the United States that Europe did have the will to add deeds to the words of the 2001 Laeken Declaration, which urged Europe to aspire to the status of a military hard power rather than only a civilian soft power. It is lamentable that, after the Iraq and Afghanistan interventions, smart-power operations – save the Atalanta anti-piracy mission in East Africa – have been limited in scope and scale.

The problem is that Europe is surrounded by a 'ring of fire' composed of military, diplomatic and demographic challenges in Russia, the Middle East and North Africa, all of which require the demonstration of active clout to deter autocratic regimes and degrade non-state actors in nearby failed states. While economic sanctions against Russia and economic pressure against Iran have yielded results, Europe's political power falls well behind its defence capacity, threatening to embolden rivals and thus eventually imperil European and British interests.

Smart-power thinking is required to resolve these issues. In order to protect its economic and diplomatic power, Europe must aspire to achieve at least regional-power status, with Britain playing a leading part. This thinking consists of four components:

(1) Application of European power as a force for good in the region. Britain and France must combine planning and resources to transform the regional environment and build a security apparatus based on the projection of democracy and the rule of law.
(2) Active willingness to use this power, supported by soft-power mechanisms.
(3) Rigorous application of (1) and (2) within the framework of a grand strategy including all NATO, EU and other European members of intergovernmental institutions.
(4) Enabling of Britain, France, Germany and Italy (the G4 leading European powers) to coordinate both their resources and all the relevant European organisations with the aim of providing an intergovernmental foreign, security and defence strategy under one roof.

With Europeans having such formidable assets at their disposal, a better means of coordinating their economic, political and military activities is required. Britain and its allies need to forge

Europe into a regional power to provide more coherent long-term thinking and political weight with which to shape the wild east and south of a continent now losing touch with the values central to their interests.

If this does not happen, the British are condemned to be haunted by the ghost of Aneurin Bevan as they walk naked into the conference chambers not only of Europe, but of the world.

A Smart Brexit 'grand strategy'

The twenty-first-century world is likely to be just as troublesome as the twentieth. New challenges to the stability of Europe stare the hobbled continental statesmen in the face. When leaders warn of a 'ring of fire' around Europe they are not indulging in outlandish rhetoric. As Jacques Delors agreed, 'future conflicts will be sparked by cultural factors rather than economics or ideology.'[8]

Islamic terrorism, fuelled by resentment against the West, represents the most obviously dangerous strategic challenge to European security, but it is perhaps the less existential one. The EU's mission creep into the civilisational fault-lines of Europe in the Balkans and Ukraine, without a consistent grand strategy – or the power to back one up – leaves it exposed to Russian revanchism. Dealing with the rise of new global political power centres with only half-hearted and often disunited economic leverage exposes Europe to the tactics of divide and rule. It doesn't help, as Ivan Kratsev said, that 'creating an EU foreign policy is like making Christmas dinner for your wife, your ex-wife and your mother-in-law and then hoping someone is still there to eat it',[9] but it speaks to an inertia and lack of geopolitical willpower which is unsustainable. The West has lost sight of the prize, namely a Europe which is a free-trade, free-market, low-unemployment, high-growth economy supported by a strong, values-driven, smart-power force. It is this objective that should focus the minds of all the players not only in London but also Paris, Berlin and Washington.

This rethink requires a return to the political Europe based on peace and security which was central to Churchill's dream. The stability achieved within the frontiers of the EU is threatened by a retreat from democratic values. The security of Europe is threatened by failure to engage coherently with the European neighbourhood. If Britain's interests in continental peace are to be upheld, how should it develop the vital strategic doctrine, institutions and levers of influence? What would a British-led 'European grand strategy' include?

First, it would be focused on reinforcing the two circles of Europe and the United States, what Timothy Garton Ash calls Euro-Atlanticism, Britain as 'a child of Europe and the parent of America'.[10] It is Britain's absolute priority to ensure that the United States and Europe are now united in dealing with the challenges outlined. A fracturing of the transatlantic military, economic and political bond would please only those rivals feeding those challenges. The so-called 'special relationship' has never been exclusive to Britain and the United States, as it was predicated on Britain playing its part in influencing the policy and direction of continental Europe. London now needs to resist isolationism and, instead, provide new impetus in practising smart engagement across the Channel, making and winning diplomatic arguments in all the bodies where European states convene. This is, after all, what many European partners are beseeching it to do.

Second, and most important, would be to make clear the values that underpin the cooperative structure. The vigorous promotion of democracy, freedom and the rule of law – enforced by economic, military and diplomatic means – must be at the heart of any grand strategy. Europe must be as agile as its rivals, not hidebound by slow-moving structures and limited diplomatic weaponry. As one of Britain's leading grand strategists, Robert Cooper, said: 'when we are operating in the jungle, we must also use the laws of the jungle'.[11] The EU's burdensome voting structure makes it an unwieldy beast in the global jungle, so it is left to Britain and France, as the key European powers, to provide the words and the deeds and provide continental leadership.

Thirdly, a grand strategy must also apply the correct structures in order for Britain and France and others to act in the wider world. The hard- and soft-power instruments require coherent delivery mechanisms, but currently there is next to no coordination between the different European international organisations operating on the continent. As the EU sought to be the dominant European actor, other more pertinent operators were sidelined and the air was sucked out of the non-economic approach to issues. In short, this approach requires three pillars of action for Britain to promote:

Pillar	*Coordinating organisation*
Security	NATO Organisation for Security and Cooperation in Europe (OSCE) European External Action Service (EEAS) Europol
Democracy	Council of Europe (CofE) Organisation for Economic Co-operation and Development (OECD)
Prosperity	European Union European Economic Area

The grand strategy of a united Europe: the Councils of Europe

To lead in the three pillars of security, democracy and prosperity, Britain needs to entrench its central role in NATO, the Council of Europe, the OSCE and in the European Single Market.

In fact, this was the core of Churchill's approach. In 1942 Churchill circulated a paper to the War Cabinet proposing that there be a European Council to establish a United States of Europe after the war. Indeed, after the first British victory of the war at El Alamein, Churchill wrote to his foreign secretary Anthony Eden on 21 October 1942: 'Hard as it is to say now … I look forward to a United States of Europe, in which the barriers between the nations will be greatly minimised and unrestricted travel will be possible.'[12]

The British government should lead in advocating a new permanent intergovernmental body called the Councils of Europe. This body will have as its governing body a European Security Council upon which will sit the European members of the G7 – Britain, Germany, France and Italy – the secretaries-general of NATO, the Council of Europe and the OSCE, and the president of the Council of the European Union. France and Germany have already proposed that there should be a European Security Council, in order to address internal and external security and defence issues facing Europe. This European Security Council should be prepared by a meeting of foreign affairs, defence and interior ministers.[13]

To add democratic legitimacy to its deliberations, united under its umbrella should be the currently disparate bodies representing European states:

- NATO Parliamentary Assembly
- Council of Europe Parliamentary Assembly
- OSCE Parliamentary Assembly
- EU Parliament.

Furthermore, the civil services of all the institutions, including the EU Commission, could be unified.

This light-touch apparatus is necessary because all these organisations suffer from a disease common to many top-level political fora: too much diplomacy and too little democracy in their procedures. With public consent at rock bottom, they cannot continue to operate side by side without close collaboration, each acting in accordance with its own particular qualities, experience and status. In a report by Klaus Hänsch, MEP, former president of the European Parliament, on the links between the major European institutions at pan-European level, he called for much closer cooperation to meet the challenges of the future. He urged the introduction of a 'system of European confederal co-operation' that would cover the Council of Europe and the Conference on Security and Co-operation in Europe, in addition to the EU.[14]

The last 50 years constitute a sufficiently long stretch of European history to enable these various institutions to determine their specific characters and individual missions in full. They write reports, all translated into several European languages and sometimes unwittingly covering almost exactly the same subjects, in spite of the opportunities offered by modern communications. All institutions have, for example, committees working on politics, culture, agriculture and the environment. Costly absurdities such as the European Parliament and the Council of Europe sharing cheek-by-jowl offices in Strasbourg, taking decisions alongside each other in almost complete isolation, as if they were each dealing with their own separate Europe, cannot continue.

In this navel-gazing world, the ultimate shared objective, a continental Europe where the same social values guarantee the freedom and happiness of its citizens, is forgotten. It is at this level that the various European organisations have to join up their mission and responsibilities towards the public and the taxpayer – an objective that will be achieved by primarily political not economic means.

In order to coordinate and promote action under these three pillars, this book recommends greater coherence across UK government in promoting British interests inside these organisations. There should be a Secretary of State for European Affairs assisted by a unit at the centre of government specifically to advise the prime minister of the smart-power actions required throughout Whitehall and Westminster in order to coordinate the grand strategy. By making tangible all relevant parts of the UK's new direction, decision-makers inside and outside government would be able to comprehend the UK's place on the European stage and promote it.

This is not a task list simply for the Foreign Office, as it is no longer the only department involved in international relations. The entire government has to think about Britain in this new environment. How does the UK retain the trust and influence deriving from its past? How does it proceed into a future where the edges of statecraft have become softer and more porous than ever before?

A strong Britain, in a strong Europe, locked into a strong Atlantic alliance working with our allies in all key international organisations, not just a few, is the best framework for preserving and furthering British influence and enhancing the country's prosperity and power. In order to protect the West, the Euro-Atlantic world of Washington, London, New York, Paris, Berlin, Rome, Madrid and Dublin needs to revive its spirit as a shield, as well as a sword, for threatened civilisational values. In an era where there is no longer any distinction between domestic and foreign policy, and in a political environment more international than ever, European security can only be secured by nation-state cooperation. Better deployment of the UK's smart power will only achieve real momentum if the UK maintains its sense of purpose. A long-term strategic narrative about the European role of the UK needs to come from the centre of government. The absolute priority is for the UK to remain a first-rank performer in the global network, and it still has every opportunity to do so. However, if the government does not shape the transformed European order, the UK will risk finding itself outwitted, out-competed, isolated and increasingly insecure.

While the continent has liberated itself from its past, Britain, 70 years after the end of World War II, still finds itself imprisoned by it. To end that trauma Britain's grand strategy needs a Churchillian new patriotism.

The three pillars

1. The democracy pillar – smart power in promoting the values of freedom, democracy and the rule of law

The Council of Europe was founded by Winston Churchill and is not an EU institution, yet it possesses the original copyright over the European twelve-star flag and Ode to Joy anthem long since pocketed by the European Commission. It has as members no less than 47 European states, and represents a form of intergovernmental co-operation in contrast to the supranational model run by the EU. It was established to entrench the wartime Four Freedoms and the United Nations Charter, which 'reaffirmed faith in fundamental human rights, and dignity and worth of the human person' and committed all member states to promote 'universal respect for, and observance of, human rights and fundamental freedoms for all without distinction as to race, sex, language, or religion'.[15]

Established under the Treaty of London in 1949, the Council of Europe represented one of the first attempts at European reconciliation and cooperation after World War II. The Council first established the Convention for the Protection of Human Rights and Fundamental Freedoms in 1950, followed by the European Court of Human Rights (ECHR) in 1959. This is the most developed regional system of human rights protection worldwide, and offers major opportunities to further the UK's human rights objectives, as well as promoting the rule of law and democracy, throughout wider Europe and beyond. Membership expanded rapidly in the 1990s; there are now 47 member states, with all European countries except Belarus, Kazakhstan and Kosovo represented. Member states agree and set standards on issues including human rights, terrorism, crime, money laundering and trafficking, by negotiating and ratifying Conventions. The UK is an active and influential member of the Council, partly because of its status as one of five major contributors to the budget.

However, the creation of the EEC in 1957 meant that the Council of Europe was sidelined from the economic actions required to create the common market. Politically, the democracy-promotion role of the Council was frozen until the fall of the Berlin Wall and the opening up of Eastern Europe. Since the collapse of the Soviet Union, it has focused its efforts on strengthening respect for human rights and the rule of law in the new democracies east of the Elbe, while the EU restricts itself to economic and monetary interests.

Even though the financial weight of the European Union is greater than that of the Council, the political dimension of the Council – supported by a secretariat of no less than 1,800 civil servants – is, nevertheless, much more comprehensive than that of the EU on account of both the size of the territory it covers and the purely political issues it deals with. And it will be primarily in the specific domains covered by the Council of Europe that Europe might achieve further cooperation over the next few decades, and thus achieve greater unity and greater stability. In this respect, the Council of Europe's agenda of human rights, democracy and the rule of law cannot succeed unless it is coordinated with other European institutions and, indeed, the member states that pay for them.

The Council of Europe comprises a Parliamentary Assembly on which sit elected representatives of the members' parliaments. Regular meetings of the Council of Foreign Ministers pass conventions and charters that recommend political actions that its members should take. Although the Council's recommendations in many areas are not binding, in the policy area of human rights it does have legal jurisdiction. Under the European Convention on Human Rights, all signatories are obliged to uphold the right to life, to protection against torture and inhumane treatment, to freedom and safety, to a fair trial, to respect for one's private family life and correspondence, and to freedom of expression. States and individuals, regardless of their nationality, may refer alleged violations to the ECHR in Strasbourg.

When the UK held the chairmanship of the Council's Committee of Ministers in 2012, it adopted the Brighton Declaration on reform of the ECHR, ensuring that the court focuses on cases that really require its attention, deals with its large backlog of cases (over 140,000) and seeks to improve the quality of its judges and judgments.

A reformed European Court of Human Rights is in the UK's national interest. In an increasingly networked world, UK security and prosperity depend to a large extent on stability and adherence to human rights across the European continent: this needs an effectively functioning court. Also, the presence of countries such as Russia, perceived to be backsliding from the Convention, enables Britain and its allies to use the Parliamentary Assembly as a more combative arena for debates on the future of Europe than the more anodyne and technocratic European Parliament of the EU.

2. *The security pillar – smart power in protecting Europe*

NATO and the EU remain unstrategic partners. Ever since the false dawn of the Berlin Plus agreements in 2003, there has been an unwillingness to provide NATO–EU relations with a grand strategy. Such a political arrangement – which would formally clarify the areas of cooperation and joint activities beyond the technicalities of existing arrangements – is required. The EU's failure to create a sustained security and defence capacity means the EU is best seen as a soft, economic power. The establishment of the European External Action Service in 2009 has hardly changed that. Nor is there any coordination between the four regional organisations – NATO, the OSCE, the Council of Europe and the EU – all of which are empowered to influence Europe's policy on peace and security.

Although there have been some 37 EU security missions since the first European Security Strategy was inaugurated in 2003, officials cannot hide their frustration with the multiplicity of competing structures and the difficulty in preparing and deploying multinational operations.

The 2016 European Security Strategy addresses this problem by seeking the 'streamlining of our institutional structure' through 'enhanced co-operation' between willing countries that 'might lead to a more structured form of co-operation, making full use of the Lisbon Treaty's potential'.[16] However, while lip service is paid to joint EU military and civilian planning headquarters and defence procurement harmonisation, there are few plans to deal with the five key threats confronting Europe first identified in the first European Security Strategy thirteen years ago:

(1) terrorism;
(2) Russian revanchism;
(3) regional conflicts in Europe's neighbourhood;
(4) state failure and corrupt governance, organised crime, illegal drugs-trading and people-trafficking.

The UK's half-hearted involvement in the EU's security and defence cooperation must now be placed in context. Smart-power thinking requires Britain to involve itself pro-actively in European defence activities whatever the nomenclature. This requires a grand strategy based on Britain leading in cooperation with France and the United States. Two circles united.

The entente amicable

In 2010 President Sarkozy visited London. On a visit more often remembered for the furore surrounding his new wife, Carla Bruni, it was in fact he who made history. First, the rhetoric of a new *entente amicable* offered a hand across the Channel to refresh an alliance moribund since 1956. Second, the reintegration of France into NATO's military command marked the end of Gaullism, and the end of French efforts to build a European defence force in competition with NATO.

By reinstating France in NATO, Sarkozy put to bed the cross-Channel suspicion that France's interests in creating a European defence policy were essentially anti-American. Britain, the 'indispensable nation' for European defence, became an ideal ally both bilaterally and under the aegis of the Atlantic Alliance. This was a reversal of de Gaulle's view that, for France to be considered a Great Power, it needed an independent foreign and defence policy anchored in its domination of European security.

All that changed with the 2010 Anglo-French Treaty. Britain and France promised to lead a 'partnership of pioneers' between them, to tackle global crises, climate change and reform of international institutions. They created 'pioneer groups' on defence – the concept that the more willing and able European states should be allowed to get on with closer cooperation without being held back by the less willing and able.

If applied with conviction, Anglo-French cooperation could be transformative. On the oceans, the Royal Navy and the French Navy are the only navies, except the United States Navy, that possess aircraft carrier battle fleets, and they have pledged to pool their aircraft carriers and maritime aircraft for national, Europe-led or NATO operations. Independent of the EU's imprimatur, these forces are deployed worldwide. Moreover, their capacities – together with the Italian Navy – are about to increase, as all three states intend to build larger aircraft carriers supported by next-generation warship and missile-bearing submarines.

In the air, both the Royal Air Force and the French Air Force are capable of overwhelming opponents. Both air forces have agreed to sign a single maintenance contract for future military aircraft made by the European Aeronautic Defence and Space Company (EADS), the A400M, in an effort to cut costs and preserve interoperability, in spite of Germany's insistence on making its own arrangements.

The Anglo-French emphasis on pioneer groups demonstrated that flexibility, not uniformity, in defence deployment is required. A multi-speed approach (from shared research to joint forces) would enable contributions from European states in coalitions of the willing. Importantly, it is understood that states that feel unable or unwilling to participate should not neutralise action, and that decision-making should be restricted to those states that have skin in the game.

This is the essence of pioneer groups – that member states who do not fulfil certain basic criteria (defence spending, rates of participation in operations, modernisation of armed forces as measured by investment per soldier) should stand aside, and let smaller and more committed groupings move ahead. As Europe is essentially a nuclear power, under the umbrella of Britain and France's strategic missile umbrella, smart power requires Britain and France to provide the military and diplomatic muscle in the region to bolster European defence and security.

The special relationship

The special relationship, forged during the war, needs to be revived as the beating heart of transatlantic cooperation. Divorcing European defence from the United States would be a mistake. As the former UK ambassador to the United States, Sir Christopher Meyer, has warned, the British would be wrong to fall into the trap of 'sentimentalising a relationship towards which the Americans have always been notably unsentimental', saying that this attitude 'can lead to the hubristic delusion that Britain, above all nations, enjoys a privileged status in Washington'.[17]

Britain and the United States certainly share values but, as Suez proved in 1956, the UK cannot expect the Americans to put our national interests first just because we talk the same language. On our continuing participation in European policy, we must not allow the view to prevail that the USA will welcome, or be indifferent to, British isolationism. The USA wants Britain to lead in Europe.

So while Britain provides one of the United States' most important relationships, of central importance to that relationship is our position in Europe. Consistency in the geopolitical position of Britain and Europe is vital on a range of issues, such as economic liberalisation, free trade and security. As Assistant Secretary Philip Gordon said:

> Britain has been such a special partner of the United States. The United Kingdom shares our values, shares our interests, and has significant resources to bring to the table. More than most

others, its voice within Europe is essential and critical to the United States.[18]

3. The prosperity pillar – smart power in creating jobs and growth throughout Europe

The European Union has always been a political project, but because it could not simply duplicate the work of the Council of Europe and the OSCE – which dealt with democracy, human rights and the rule of law – it had to focus on areas where other organisations were less active, namely economic and financial interests. The Single Market is the greatest success of this approach.

Following the Brexit vote, how should Britain keep its trade links with the EU alive while retaining its seat at the table where the rules are made? We are at the beginning of a long and winding road to a possible complete divorce – a hard Brexit – in which quitting the Single Market is the nuclear option. While there is no question that the Single Market is only sustainable if countries apply large sections of the acquis (European law), many countries – inside and outside the EU – have significant trading links to Britain that flourish within the Single Market.

If the UK is to leave the EU, it makes more sense to amend an existing model than to try to carve out a completely new economic relationship. The European Economic Area (EEA), established on 1 January 1994, fits the bill. It was aimed, as the then president of the European Commission, Jacques Delors, stated, 'to have positive effects on the economy of the continent as a whole ... likely to produce new economies of scale and to boost competitiveness, as did the completion of the Single Market amongst the 12 Member States of the European Union'.[19]

The EEA already consists of the 28 EU member states plus Norway, Iceland and Liechtenstein. Were Turkey to be asked to join, there would be a total of 32 states and a single market of over 600 million people. This would not only be the biggest single market in the world, it would unite the entire continent of Europe. When Churchill made his last speech about Europe at London's Central Hall, Westminster, in July 1957 – some four months after six founding nations established the European Economic Community – he welcomed the formation of a 'common market' provided only that 'the whole of free Europe will have access.'

Importantly, for those that would be prepared to abandon in full Britain's position in the Single Market, much that would be lost with a hard Brexit would be retained if a reformed EEA could be achieved. The EEA covers other important areas such as research and development, education, the environment, consumer protection and tourism. It also guarantees equal rights and obligations within the internal market for citizens and businesses in the EEA.

The EEA Agreement does not cover the Common Agricultural and Common Fisheries policies, the customs union, the Common Trade Policy, the Common Foreign and Security Policy, justice and home affairs or monetary union (EMU).

Britain should seek the assistance of all the existing EU member states to craft anew the economic and political shape of this larger single market. It needs to enable those countries within the Eurozone who wish to integrate further and to allow those countries who do not to remain in a restructured single market based on the EEA model. It would adopt as its core the existing EU Single Market legislation, but with greater flexibility on the free movement of labour.

As former foreign secretary David Owen has argued:

> The legitimate safeguard of treaty change by unanimity, which has been built in from the start of the Common Market, would continue with the aim of broadly presenting two reworked treaties: one for a continuing European Union, the other for a European Community-wide single market.[20]

For this to happen without legalistic arguments, challenges to the interpretation of the treaties and allegations of bad faith, all European countries must be involved as equals in an agreed restructuring of the European polity.

First, all European states should remain full members of a single market based on the EU's existing acquis communautaire, within a larger, separate organisation. It should be governed by qualified majority voting based on a wider single market and customs union. As David Owen proposed, this grouping of 32 states or more could be called the European Community, funded and controlled by all its member states and operating under the European Council. It could have its own secretary general and parliamentary representation. If the EEA were made flexible enough to provide access to the Single Market but a) not require membership of the euro, and b) allow some reciprocal limitations on free movement, it could provide an answer for the UK and potentially other states hostile to further integration. If their security interests were sufficiently assured, the Baltic States, Sweden, Denmark and Poland as well as the Balkans might find this the most practical and least constraining group to belong to. For all players, maintaining the Single Market is the essence of a 'win-win' solution. The EU cannot expand indefinitely, but the Single Market can continue to grow around its frontiers.

Second, what will also emerge as part of this restructuring is a Eurozone whose economic, fiscal and monetary policies will develop in ways that involve, in essence, a single government. This may be acceptable for most but not all of the existing Eurozone countries. Countries with interests that are too divergent to accommodate may avoid the core of European integration and opt out, preferring instead membership of the EEA that allows them to participate fully in the Single Market, or to negotiate a free-trade agreement. The Eurozone countries which remain would continue to be called the European Union.

Through this device, the unhappy coexistence of the Eurozone and the Single Market would be resolved. Those member states content to pool their economic sovereignty could do so in a post-Maastricht European Union; those content with the virtues of the Single Market could do so in, as Owen seeks, a pre-Maastricht European Community.

Is the Single Market dispensable?

The UK economy benefits substantially from the Single Market – which according to HM Treasury and Department of Business analysis is worth some £11 trillion. While making a net contribution of £6.9 billion to the EU budget, the British economy benefits from the Single Market alone by up to £90 billion, or £3,300 per household every year. The Single Market has enabled wider choice and lower prices for the consumer, higher inward investment, and significant economies of scale for UK manufacturers. While leaving the EU would not stop all trade with Europe, Britain's ability to shape the regulations and rules for that £90 billion of benefits is vital. Since some Single Market rules might be bad for UK businesses, Britain requires diplomatic and commercial skill to propose, veto or reform them.

Has the Single Market been good for Britain's economy?

Since trade between EU member states is tariff-free, the EU has focused on the non-tariff barriers to trade that arise from 28 different sets of national regulations. It has done so by creating common minimum standards and by getting member states to recognise each other's rules. Britain's Single Market membership has boosted its trade in goods with other member states by 55 per cent. The Single Market has also boosted investment flows between Britain and the rest of the EU. In 1997, other EU member states accounted for 30 per cent of the accumulated stock of foreign direct investment in Britain. By 2012, they accounted for 50 per cent.

Critics of the Single Market point to the fact that Britain's trade with emerging economies is growing faster than with the EU. Some argue that this shows that the Single Market is no longer important. However, some, though not all, emerging economies are growing quicker than Europe because they have unused resources to deploy. Moreover, there is no evidence of trade diversion or that membership of the Single Market has reduced its trade with non-EU countries.

A report from the Centre for European Reform, 'The Economic Consequences of Leaving the EU', notes that about half of UK exports go to the EU while only about a tenth of EU exports come to the UK. However, the key fact is that the UK's economic future with Europe is not about the negotiation of tariffs on products at borders. The real issue with the post-Brexit economy is that a lot of trade is in components and parts of finished products. Therefore it is not tariffs but regulations, standards, licensing, authorisations and professional qualifications which represent the invisible but, for trade, deadly barriers between Britain and its European customers and suppliers that the Single Market has stripped away by merging them into a single European framework.

British business – big, medium and small – needs a settlement which provides long-term, predictable and unhindered European supply chains and distribution networks. Only by maintaining this regime will Britain remain as the ideal base for business to trade onwards into the Single Market.

The problem for the future is not only the trade-off with free movement of people but the fact that non-tariff barriers cannot be identified or legally removed unless Britain remains in the room where regulations are made.

Does Single Market regulation tie up the British economy in red tape?

Is it worth being in the room anyway? There can be little doubt that some of the Single Market's regulations impose more costs than benefits. But the idea that such regulation adds up to a major supply-side problem is wrong. The first reason is that common rule-making is vital to the very existence of the Single Market. If the UK declared war on red tape, divergent rules would emerge between the Single Market and the UK, and exporters would pay the price in higher compliance costs. However, exclusion from the Single Market would not merely lead to confusion over regulatory equivalence; it would also imperil the scale that an economic space of 500 million consumers provides. Big domestic markets allow their companies to grow quickly and take a strong global position.

The debate about red tape also misses the point that, according to the OECD, the UK is the second-least-regulated product market in Europe, behind only the Netherlands. Its labour market restrictions are no more burdensome than those in the US, Canada or Australia, and are far less so than in other continental European countries. So Single Market rules do not impose severe harmonisation across Europe; the UK retains its deregulated markets, despite its Single Market membership. So escaping Single Market rules would not lead to higher output – in fact, the most likely result is that exit would lead to lower output. If leaving the Single Market leads to higher trade costs, then the UK economy will be damaged.

The question is whether trade arrangements outside the Single Market would be worse than inside. Outside the Single Market, market access would be more difficult. Since market access is important to British prosperity, it would be a very difficult bargain. But if the City still wants full access to the EU's financial markets, it would have to accept services and capital rules. So, the Brexit gavotte leads Britain and its businesses back to square one, but with less power over regulation, not more. The only sensible option is to achieve full, not piecemeal, access to the Single Market through a modernised EEA. This is a mission critical for British prosperity.

Prosperity in action

What is being proposed in completing the Single Market and increasing Europe's competitiveness has a great bearing on future developments in the UK. To create new and innovative businesses, Britain cannot forsake leadership in four new single markets.

1. *Energy market*

Energy security is one of the key policy issues both for energy suppliers and the governments that need to keep the lights on, reduce energy bills and cut greenhouse gas emissions. Interconnection – the cross-border transmission of gas or electricity capacity – is a policy that achieves all three outcomes. The purpose of these infrastructure linkages is to reduce dependency on single providers and monopolies. Governments also need to concentrate on the regulatory side of the equation in order to complete the integration of the European energy market.

Eliminating regulatory barriers and anti-competitive business practices is never very popular, but the conformity of national measures with the EU's Third Energy Package, which was adopted in 2009, is critical to energy security. European Commission reports identify where the problems lie in energy market integration and linkages: there is a lack of urgency in certain EU member states who prefer to protect narrow national interests.

Without coordination, European countries intent on realising the benefits of interconnection could end up building more cables than are needed at great expense, ending up with a less efficient system. The opportunity of the UK and other EU member states for greater interconnection is profound. But to avoid wasting taxpayers' money in the pursuit of this prize, there is a strong need for greater coordination across the continent.

2. *Digital market (telecoms and digital sectors)*

There is an area of high growth that, if encouraged properly, could set us on track for moving once again towards a higher productivity trajectory. This is the digital economy, where development in the UK has been extraordinary. All countries in Europe are looking for ways to stimulate and maintain growth. Completing the Digital Single Market is an oft-heard call demand, including from the British government. So why is it important? The internet and digital technology have changed all our lives: how we communicate, do business, work and learn, as well as our social interactions. Yet much of this activity is confined within our national boundaries. British consumers can only buy mobile phone services from companies in the UK. They cannot download films from another member state. And small and medium-sized enterprises (SMEs) in particular are not using the full potential of the internet for their sales. As a result, the EU is lagging behind other parts of the world: the digital economy accounts for 4 per cent of the EU economy compared to 6 per cent in the USA and 7 per cent in China. Only 14 per cent of SMEs use the internet for selling online, against a target of 33 per cent by 2015. And only 12 per cent of consumers are buying online across borders. Studies have shown that a digital single market could increase European GDP by 4 per cent by 2020. It will create jobs, increase choice and boost innovation. The Commission's forecasts are that this will add up to £340 billion of growth in Europe over the next ten years and create hundreds of thousands of new jobs. How can we make it happen?

Creating a telecoms union

Investment in wireless broadband lags behind those in Asia and the USA. European equipment vendors are outflanked on their own turf by their Chinese counterparts. The service offered to mobile consumers, though improved by roaming regulation, will still lag behind, in consistency and coverage conditions on the continent, what customers can now get in the USA, Japan and China. All this reflects a lack of doctrine and vision for the benefits that a single market for European telecommunications could bring. It is clear that market fragmentation prevents European carriers from capturing economies of scale and scope. The United States' two biggest telecoms carriers are each larger than the three largest European carriers combined. European consumers are worse off as a result. There are big operators in Europe: Vodafone from the UK, Orange from France, Telefónica from Spain, Deutsche Telekom from Germany and Telecom Italia. But they do not want to confront governments and regulators, preferring to play the multi-domestic game and take modest advantage of market fragmentation.

Britain should call for all stakeholders – telecommunications managers, administrations, bankers – to build the European telecommunications single market into an industry powerhouse, for the benefit of all industries and citizens.

Creating the Digital Single Market

Europe, and particularly the UK, with its strengths in the digital and creative industries, could benefit from the completion of a digital single market. The European Commission has a wide-ranging ambition covering Internet access and infrastructure, but also associated issues such as data protection, copyright, data security and the allocation of spectrum. Britain is pushing for regulation to be modernised, and must ensure there is an appropriate regulatory framework that supports and facilitates cross-border services. Enabling pan-European services can help reduce the regulatory burden of more than 28 different sets of rules.

The UK and its businesses should continue to play a substantial part in the Digital Single Market and shape the standards that may be adopted across Europe. In truth, the digital economy has been a great UK success story, and successive governments have made it a priority in their industrial strategy.

But the fear is that full understanding of digital's contribution is still lacking. Work published by the National Institute for Economic and Social Research (NIESR) in 2013 calculated that the digital economy probably contributed significantly more to the British economy than previously considered, employing not just 167,000 people, as the Office for National Statistics thought, but the much larger number of just under 500,000.

The digital sector consists not just of lots of small start-ups, making no or very little money, as is the popular perception. Instead, as the NIESR report highlighted, the sector spreads across many businesses, including larger ones, and also across many regions of the economy, not just London. The report also found that it was one of the most dynamic and fast-growing areas of the economy, and had at the time been expanding some 22 per cent faster than traditional firms. Broadband connectivity, where more investment has been announced, is key, but so are ecosystems across the country that can link academia, entrepreneurship and innovative activities of smaller firms in a way that supports the adoption of new ways of doing business and connecting to the customer.

Britain needs to be part of – and driving – the digital agenda. And the only way for us to do this is by remaining within the Single Market.

3. *Capital market*

The 2008 financial crisis tossed the City of London's reputation in the gutter. Yet after a period of regulatory overhaul, London remains Europe's pre-eminent financial centre. That position is crucial to sustaining jobs and growth not just in the UK but across the continent.

Britain remaining in the Single Market is vital for the financial sector. Access to it and the web of Europe-wide regulation are fundamentally intertwined with the UK's attractiveness as a place for international banks to set up their European and global headquarters. The industry now has an estimated trade surplus with Europe of £15.2 billion.

But uncertainty over the UK's new relationship with Europe and the prospect of banking union among Eurozone members loom large as risks that could make London less attractive as an international centre across many industries, not just financial and professional services. Economically, the survival of the Eurozone is in the national interest since nearly half of UK exports of goods and services are to the EU. As nations in the Eurozone try to push towards closer fiscal and political integration, the need for the UK to have a coherent strategy towards the European Union will only intensify.

How close are we to having a single market in financial services? A 2009 study by CRA International, 'Evaluation of the Economic Impact of the FSAP', pointed to a 90 per cent reduction in the cost of cross-border retail payments. However, there are still gaps. The fact that progress has been made is in no small part due to UK involvement and leadership in that area. Key aspects of European financial services law are modelled on that of the UK. Despite that progress, capital markets in Europe are roughly half as developed as in the USA, relative to the size of the economy.

Over the past five years, European companies would have been able to raise an additional $1 trillion a year in the capital markets over and above what they actually raised if markets in Europe were as deep as those in the USA. So the challenge now is to develop the market in financial services by developing a capital markets union which would present a significant opportunity for UK financial services. In its simplest form, a capital markets union is about breaking down the many barriers and obstacles across Europe that are holding back the free flow of capital across borders to where it can be most effectively invested and deployed. In doing so, a capital markets union could expand the pool of available funding for businesses and infrastructure projects, help wean the European economy off its over-reliance on bank lending, and provide more opportunities for individuals and pension schemes to invest their money for the long term.

The goals are to finance jobs and growth throughout Europe and to have a financial system that is better able to absorb shocks. Banks are shrinking, and so cannot do the job of funding economic expansion on their own. Nor are they good at coping with crises. The solution is to increase non-bank finance – including shares and bonds – and to integrate further Europe's capital markets. That will lead to greater critical mass and lower financing costs, as well as soften the blow of an economic shock by sharing the pain across a wider area, provided risk is really transferred from bank balance sheets.

Europe is increasingly playing a role in the implementation of agreed G20, Financial Stability Board and Basel financial arrangements. The UK is a member of these organisations in its own right, and must increase its influence in achieving capital markets union. Perhaps where banking and the financial markets went wrong before the crisis was in forgetting that their primary purpose is to support and service the rest of the economy. If capital markets union can help restore that purpose, and help reconnect those companies and projects that need capital with those that have it and want to invest it, then it may prove to be one of the more valuable British leadership projects.

4. Science market

The global financial crisis demonstrated that diversification away from finance is needed for a stable and competitive future. The promise of science lies in its proven capacity to drive economies, as in the well-documented cases of Finland and South Korea. The USA also, despite its 'small government' rhetoric, has driven its tech industry to huge success by allocating public funds for innovation.

There is ample data showing that the return on investment for research and innovation is substantial. Strong science creates well-paid, high-growth jobs. This investment can be targeted at solving the energy, health and environmental problems that we need to crack for a sustainable future. So it is not just about economic growth, but also the type of society, economy and environment we want to live in.

Europe provides a common economic space within which talent can move freely. It enlarges Britain's research base. Whereas the UK's science budget has stagnated over many years, shrinking our real-terms investment down to the bottom of the G7, Europe has ramped up its science spend. The UK secures a disproportionate amount of EU research, development and innovation funding – over £6 billion, or 15.5 per cent, of the funding allocated – and every £1 of such funding has been calculated to increase the added value to industry by £13.

In 2014, despite a reduced overall budget, the EU ramped up its science spend by 30 per cent to develop a new seven-year research and innovation programme, called Horizon 2020, funded to the tune of nearly £80 billion. The programme supports researcher mobility, multinational collaborative projects, academia–business interaction and a lot of small innovative businesses.

The nature of EU research funding means that it complements and adds value to national structures, enabling projects individual member states could not undertake alone. And, because of the high reputation of British researchers, we are able to influence the European agenda. Europe is the world's largest knowledge economy and has access to international networks, as well as global significance and direct influence over the regulatory environment. British academics, researchers and students move freely across national frontiers within compatible, comparable and coherent European higher education systems. Over 80 per cent of the UK's internationally co-authored papers are written with European partners.

Knowledge is by nature international and without boundaries. In an increasingly global society and economy, the internationalisation of higher education is not only inevitable, it is essential. International collaboration is vital for the quality, competitiveness and impact of UK research, the employability of UK graduates and the success of UK universities. In this context, it is vital that the UK and its higher education sector continue to be internationally orientated and that we act to maintain, articulate and enhance a European presence for UK universities.

Conclusion

So this is the fresh start for Britain to lead Europe in challenging times. I end at the beginning, by uniting smart power and Churchill's three circles to create an approach to Europe that is both old and new. By expanding the Single Market with a focus on boosting the energy, digital, finance and science industries, and by championing the Councils of Europe, charged with uniting the many strands of intergovernmental cooperation, all around a grand strategy to promote democracy, security and prosperity on the continent, Britain could once more achieve leadership in Europe. 'If we rise to the occasion,' as Churchill said, 'it may be found that once again we hold the key to opening a safe and happy future to humanity, and will gain for ourselves gratitude and fame.'[21]

The British problem

This means ending the push-me-pull-you gambits the British have used to harness the power of the English-speaking world and Europe in the past:

- Joseph Chamberlain's three circles were defeated by the Empire's weakness and World War II.
- Churchill's three circles were defeated by imperial nostalgia and a failure of leadership.
- Thatcher's three circles were defeated by German reunification and the poison of apartheid.
- Blair's three circles were defeated by Iraq, the euro and the Constitution.

But it was not only history that impeded progress. The real failure was of political imagination and will. The Foreign Office hit the nail on the head when identifying why, despite the positivity of the renewed British vision, a dialogue of the deaf was emerging in the Europe of the 1990s. Britain's ambassador to Germany said:

> You would think that [with the experience of Margaret Thatcher and the success of the British economy] Britain would be giving the lead in Europe and the continentals would be following it. But is this happening? I think not. Why not? Because we don't seem to be interested in any particular objective other than the internal market. What I think is missing: Vision. I would plead that more thought be given to the style of British policy in Europe. Kohl said to me that in any political argument one should bear in mind not only the current battle but the next.[22]

Lord Hannay, former UK permanent representative to the EU, echoed the need for a 'vision thing' while realistically recognising that all member states sabotage cooperative European successes so as to appear to have singly defended their national interests. How then to explain the conundrum at the heart of the growing disconnect between Britain's active engagement and its perception of failure?

He said:

> Our problem is that we are more effective in blocking other people's ideas than in putting forward ideas of our own. There is a market for ideas. The more we can generate positive suggestions, the less we will find ourselves reacting defensively to other people's.[23]

The European problem

For the EU, the solution cannot be simply to carry on as usual. This is the moment for thorough self-reflection on the future of the European project. The EU was based on the idea that economic integration reduces conflict. By linking European economies together – first in the form of the European Coal and Steel Community, later in the Common Market and the euro – the European project hoped to bind them together so closely that war between the states of Europe would be inconceivable. This economic imperative then created further political incentives towards a European superstate. This idea, however logical, is now being challenged in a fundamental way by both the departure of the UK and the centrifugal forces of disintegration. So the question needs to be asked: what sort of Europe is worth fighting for today?

While introspection is the EU's usual reflex, the threats facing Europe cannot be resolved by institutional tinkering, not least because, for national governments, many of these issues are existential. None of today's foreign policy challenges can be solved by governments acting alone. For the EU, Brexit will have changed the way partners, allies, rivals and citizens see the EU – and the assessment will not be encouraging.

The EU has already sought further unity in foreign, defence and economic policy, but research for Pew demonstrates a majority of Europe's citizens are indifferent to such grand designs. The crises from 2011 have hit member states and peoples in a fundamental way. Without any sense of solidarity there is no automatic instinct to develop a common response. Far from seeking more Schuman, they need more Churchill. European institutions must be coordinated better to uphold the nation states of Europe; they should not be pushing for more centralisation.

The British and European solution

Only a pan-continental view of Europe including all European states is capable of meeting the challenges facing a continent in danger. Through the existence and specific characteristics of NATO, the EU, the OSCE and the Council of Europe, the various member countries of each organisation have an opportunity to participate at different levels of European integration. Prosperity, security and democracy can only be guaranteed if the various major European organisations assume their responsibilities in a spirit of mutual openness and collaboration, and realise that better coordination of their respective activities can only strengthen their effectiveness.

This is why the Councils of Europe body must exist – to prevent continental Europe from becoming an enormous, unrecognisable, bureaucratic, inaccessible and cumbersome machine, whose civil values may perhaps still shine from the solemn declarations displayed in entry halls, but the European citizen no longer sees in action. It is what European citizens expect from their elected representatives and civil servants.

Britain must not remain passive any longer, reacting only the proposals of others. It should lead while leaving. Where the UK can act with others, so much the better; but Britain must have the confidence to set out its design for Europe – a wider Europe and a deeper Europe, living alongside and in harmony with each other.

Brexit will open up all kinds of possibilities. Contrary to the views of those who have long seen the UK as a blockage to deeper European integration, it will not necessarily deliver a more integrated EU, but may actually arrest centrifugal tendencies. It is therefore in the interest of both the UK and the EU – and of European security more generally – to ensure that a close and mutually beneficial relationship between London and Brussels results from Brexit, and that power is balanced to the benefit of both. Europe now sits at a historic crossroads: the future will depend on the political and strategic decisions taken in London, Paris, Berlin and Brussels over the next few years.

In August 1949, at the first meeting of the Council of Europe in Strasbourg, Churchill delivered his keynote speech to a thousand people, and said:

> We are reunited here, in this new Assembly, not as representatives of our several countries or various political parties, but as Europeans forging ahead, hand in hand, and if necessary elbow to elbow, to restore the former glories of Europe. There is no reason for us not to succeed in achieving our goal and laying the foundation of a United Europe. A Europe whose moral design will win the respect and acknowledgement of all humanity, and whose physical strength will be such that no person will dare to disturb it as it marches peacefully towards the future.[24]

Britain needs a fresh start every bit as much as Europe. Smart power requires imagination to forge that new path. For a West divided, a nation adrift and a continent in crisis, the solution is a revival of Churchill's three circles and a United Europe based on new foundations. With or without Brexit, the time for this has come. For the people, the path forward is a new patriotism in which the zeal of our forefathers can be applied to building, not destroying, our vital place in our continent's history.

Notes

Introduction

1. Portland Communications, 'The Soft Power 30 Index', http://softpower30.portland-communications.com/ranking.
2. See Nick Kent (ed.), *British Influence Scorecard 2015* (London: British Influence, 2015).
3. Joseph Nye, *Soft Power: The Means to Success in World Politics* (New York: Public Affairs, 2004), p. 32.

1. Pride

1. David Dilks (ed.), *Retreat from Power: Studies in Britain's Foreign Policy of the Twentieth Century, Vol. I: 1906–1939* (London: Macmillan, 1981).
2. Hugo Young, *This Blessed Plot: Britain and Europe from Churchill to Blair* (London: Macmillan, 1998).
3. Stuart Ball (ed.), *The Conservative Party since 1945* (Manchester: Manchester University Press, 1998), p. 143.
4. Oliver Franks, *Reith Lectures: Britain and the Tide of World Affairs* (1954), BBC Home Service, 7 November.
5. David Seawright, *The British Conservative Party and One Nation Politics* (London: Continuum, 2010).
6. See Douglas Hurd, *Choose Your Weapons: The British Foreign Secretary: 200 Years of Argument, Success and Failure* (London: Phoenix, 2011).
7. William Roger Louis (ed.), *Adventures with Britannia: Personalities, Politics, and Culture in Britain* (London: I.B.Tauris, 1995), p. 148 *et seq.*

8. Quoted in Peter Clarke, *The Last Thousand Days of the British Empire: The Demise of a Superpower* (London: Penguin, 2008).
9. Quoted in Peter R. Mansoor & Williamson Murray (eds), *Grand Strategy and Military Alliances* (Cambridge: Cambridge University Press, 2016), p. 154.
10. Quoted in Dianne Kirby, 'Divinely Sanctioned: The Anglo-American Cold War Alliance and the Defence of Western Civilization and Christianity, 1945–48', *Journal of Contemporary History*, 35(3) (2000), p. 385.
11. Quoted in Alasdair Blair, *Britain and the World since 1945* (London: Routledge, 2014), p. 43.
12. See Nicholas White, *Decolonisation: The British Experience since 1945* (London: Routledge, 2014).
13. Sir Reginald Coupland (ed.), *The War Speeches of William Pitt* (Oxford: Clarendon Press, 1915), p. 351.
14. Marc Trachtenberg, *A Constructed Peace: The Making of the European Settlement, 1945–1963* (Oxford: Princeton University Press, 1999), p. 116.
15. See Josef Becker & Franz Knipping (eds), *Power in Europe? Great Britain, France, Italy, and Germany in a Postwar World, 1945–1950* (New York: W. de Gruyter, 1986).
16. Quoted in Kirby, 'Divinely Sanctioned', p. 407.
17. Quoted in David Reynolds, *From World War to Cold War: Churchill, Roosevelt, and the International History of the 1940s* (Oxford: Oxford University Press, 2006).
18. See Sally Rohan, *The Western European Union: International Politics between Alliance and Integration* (London: Routledge, 2014).
19. See D. R. Thorpe, *Eden: The Life and Times of Anthony Eden First Earl of Avon, 1897–1977* (London: Vintage, 2011).
20. Sean Greenwood, *Britain and European Integration since the Second World War* (Manchester: Manchester University Press, 1996), p. 78.
21. Quoted in Mark Baimbridge, *The 1975 Referendum on Europe – Volume 1: Reflections of the Participants* (Luton: Andrews UK, 2015), p. 1958.
22. Greenwood, *Britain and European Integration*, p. 78.

23. Paul-Henri Spaak, *The Continuing Battle: Memoirs of a European, 1936–1966* (trans. Henry Fox) (London: Weidenfeld & Nicolson, 1971), p. 214.
24. Quoted in Philip Murphy, *Party Politics and Decolonization: The Conservative Party and British Colonial Policy in Tropical Africa, 1951–1964* (Oxford: Clarendon Press, 1995), p. 171.
25. Quoted in Becker & Knipping, *Power in Europe?*
26. Quoted in John Baylis, *The Diplomacy of Pragmatism: Britain and the Formation of NATO, 1942–1949* (Kent, OH: Kent State University Press, 1993), p. 120.
27. Quoted in Mark Curtis, *The Great Deception: Anglo-American Power and World Order* (London: Pluto Press, 1998), p. 18.
28. Quoted in John Baylis (ed.), *Anglo-American Relations since 1939: The Enduring Alliance* (Manchester: Manchester University Press, 1997), p. 64.
29. Quoted in George W. Ball, *The Discipline of Power: Essentials of a Modern World Structure* (London: Bodley Head, 1968), p. 79.

2. Prejudice

1. Quoted in Andrew Mullen, *The British Left's 'Great Debate' on Europe* (London: Continuum, 2007), p. 67.
2. Douglas Evans, *While Britain Slept: The Selling of the Common Market* (London: Gollancz, 1975), p. 81.
3. Richard Aldous & Sabine Lee (eds.), *Harold Macmillan and Britain's World Role* (Basingstoke: Macmillan, 1995), p. 139.
4. Desmond Dinan, *Europe Recast: A History of European Union* (Basingstoke: Palgrave Macmillan, 2014), p. 21.
5. Quoted in Lionel Bell, *The Throw that Failed: Britain's Original Application to Join the Common Market* (London: New European Publications, 1995), p. 156.
6. Quoted in Baimbridge, *The 1975 Referendum on Europe – Volume 1*, p. 1960.
7. Jussi M. Hanhimäki & Odd Arne Westad, *The Cold War: A History in Documents and Eyewitness Accounts* (Oxford: Oxford University Press, 2003), p. 327.
8. Martin Rosenbaum (ed.), *Britain and Europe: The Choices We Face* (Oxford: Oxford University Press, 2001), p. 6.

9. See Mark Baimbridge (ed.), *The 1975 Referendum on Europe – Volume 2: Current Analysis and Lessons for the Future* (Luton: Andrews UK, 2015).
10. Charles de Gaulle, Élysée Palace press conference, 14 January 1963.
11. See Stephen Wall, *The Official History of Britain and the European Community, Vol. II: From Rejection to Referendum, 1963–1975* (London: Routledge, 2012).
12. Mark Baimbridge (ed.), *The 1975 Referendum on Europe, Volume 2: Current Analysis and Lessons for the Future* (Exeter: Imprint Academic, 2006).
13. HM Government, 'The United Kingdom and the European Communities', Cm 4715, 1971.
14. Quoted in Martin Loughlin, *Sword and Scales: An Examination of the Relationship between Law and Politics* (Oxford: Hart, 2000).
15. Quoted in John Campbell, *The Iron Lady: Margaret Thatcher: From Grocer's Daughter to Iron Lady* (London: Vintage, 2012), p. 80.
16. Hugo Young, *This Blessed Plot: Britain and Europe from Churchill to Blair* (London: Macmillan, 1998), p. 306, cited in David Baker & Pauline Schnapper, *Britain and the Crisis of the European Union* (Basingstoke: Palgrave Macmillan, 2015).
17. Quoted in Trevor Salmon & Sir William Nicoll, *Building European Union: A Documentary History and Analysis* (Manchester: Manchester University Press, 1997), p. 210.
18. See John Campbell, *Roy Jenkins: A Well-Rounded Life* (London: Jonathan Cape, 2014), p. 527 *et seq.*
19. John Campbell, *The Iron Lady: Margaret Thatcher: From Grocer's Daughter to Iron Lady* (London: Vintage, 2012).
20. David Reynolds, *Britannia Overruled: British Policy and World Power in the Twentieth Century* (London: Longman, 1991), p. 271, cited in Andrew Mullen, *The British Left's 'Great Debate' on Europe*, p. 91.
21. Campbell, *The Iron Lady*, p. 416.
22. Campbell, *The Iron Lady*.
23. See European Council, 'Conclusions of the Presidency of the Proceedings of the European Council – Stuttgart, 17 to 19 June' 1983.

24. Margaret Thatcher, 'Foreword to Conservative European Manifesto', 21 May 1984.
25. See David Gowland & Arthur Turner, *Britain and European Integration, 1945–1998: A Documentary History* (London: Routledge, 2000), p. 173 *et seq.*
26. See Giovanni Moro (ed.), *The Single Currency and European Citizenship: Unveiling the Other Side of the Coin* (New York: Bloomsbury Academic, 2013).
27. Committee for the Study of Economic and Monetary Union, 'Report on economic and monetary union in the Economic Community', http://ec.europa.eu/economy_finance/publications/publication6161_en.pdf.
28. See Stephen Wall, *A Stranger in Europe: Britain and the EU from Thatcher to Blair* (Oxford: Oxford University Press, 2008), p. 63.
29. *Ibid.*, p. 46.
30. Margaret Thatcher, 'Speech at Franco-British Council Dinner', 30 November 1984.
31. Wall, *A Stranger in Europe*, p. 45.
32. Margaret Thatcher, 'The Bruges Speech', College of Europe, 1988.
33. See Winston Churchill, *Onwards to Victory* (London: Cassell & Company, 1943).
34. European Commission, 'The Commission's programme for 1990: Address by Jacques Delors, President of the Commission, to the European Parliament and his reply to the debate', *Bulletin of the European Communities Supplement*, 1(90), 17 January 1990, p. 11.
35. See Simon Bulmer, 'New Labour, New European Policy? Blair, Brown and Utilitarian Supranationalism', *Parliamentary Affairs*, 61(4) (2008), pp. 597–620.
36. Tony Blair, speech to the European Parliament, Brussels, 23 June 2005.
37. Quoted in Philip Stephens, 'The Blair Government and Europe', *Political Quarterly*, 72(1) (2001), pp. 67–75, p. 67 in Andrew Chadwick & Richard Heffernan (eds.), *The New Labour Reader* (Cambridge: Polity Press, 2003), p. 253.

38. Vernon Bogdanor, *From New Jerusalem to New Labour: British Prime Ministers from Attlee to Blair* (London: Palgrave Macmillan, 2010), p. 34.

3. Power

1. Jeremy Black, *The Tory World: Deep History and the Tory Theme in British Foreign Policy, 1679-2014* (Aldershot: Ashgate Publishing, 2015), p. 217.
2. Niall Ferguson, 'Europe must stop fighting itself', *Telegraph*, 24 June 2007, http://www.telegraph.co.uk/comment/personal-view/3640831/Europe-must-stop-fighting-itself.html.
3. Antonio Gramsci, *Selections from the Prison Books*, ed. and trans. Quintin Hoare and Geoffrey Nowell Smith (New York: International Publishers, 1971), p. 276.
4. Franklin D. Roosevelt, 'State of the Union Speech 1941', http://fdr4freedoms.org/.
5. Carroll Quigley, *The Evolution of Civilizations: An Introduction to Historical Analysis* (Indianapolis, IN: Liberty Fund, 1979).
6. Ibid., pp. 138–9.
7. Sam Perlo-Freeman, Aude Fleurant, Pieter Wezeman and Siemon Wezeman, 'Trends in World Military Expenditure, 2015', SIPRI Fact Sheet, April 2016.
8. Mark Jeurgensmeyer, *Thinking Globally: A Global Studies Reader* (London: University of California Press, 2014), p. 203.
9. Ryan Heath, 'Brussels Playbook', Politico, 29 August 2016, http://www.politico.eu/newsletter/playbook/politico-brussels-playbook-back-to-school-apple-in-commissions-eye-estonia-sort-of-votes/.
10. Timothy Garton Ash, *Free World: America, Europe, and the Surprising Future of the West* (New York: Vintage, 2005), p. 58.
11. Robert Cooper, 'The new liberal imperialism', Guardian, 7 April 2002, https://www.theguardian.com/world/2002/apr/07/1.
12. Hardev Singh Choprah, *De Gaulle and European Unity* (New Delhi: Abhinav, 1971), p. 168.
13. See https://www.auswaertiges-amt.de/EN/Europa/Aktuell/160624-BM-AM-FRA_ST.html.
14. European Parliament, 20 January 1993.

15. United Nations, 'Charter of the United Nations', 24 October 1945.
16. European Union, 'European Security Strategy 2016', June 2016.
17. Christopher Meyer, 'Our special relationship hangs by a thread', *Telegraph*, 15 January 2015, http://www.telegraph.co.uk/news/politics/11345045/Our-special-relationship-hangs-by-a-thread.html.
18. House of Commons, 'Leaving the EU', Research Paper 13/42, July 2013.
19. Therese Blanchet, Risto Piiponen and Maria Westman-Clement, *The Agreement on the European Economic Area (EEA): A Guide to the Free Movement of Goods and Competition Rules* (Oxford: Clarendon Press, 1994), Foreword.
20. David Owen, 'Labour must align with the British people on Europe before it's too late', New Statesmen, 6 June 2012, http://www.newstatesman.com/politics/politics/2012/06/labour-must-align-british-people-europe-it%E2%80%99s-too-late.
21. Richard Davis, 'The Geometry of Churchill's "Three Majestic Circles": Keystone of British Foreign Policy or *trompe l'œil*?', in Mélanie Torrent and Claire Sanderson (eds), *Challenges to British Power Status: Foreign Policy and Diplomacy in the 20th Century* (Bussels: Peter Lang, 2013) pp. 79–92.
22. Wall, *A Stranger in Europe*, pp. 76–7.
23. Ibid., p. 77.
24. Winston Churchill, Council of Europe speech, Strasbourg, August 1949.

Index